I0528643

Start Today

Be Awesome. Be You.

Jesse S. Smith

Tomis Press

Start Today: Be Awesome. Be You.
Jesse S. Smith
©2024 Jesse S. Smith
Tomis Press
Silverton, OR

Although correct to the best of the author's ability and awareness, this book is not intended as legal advice, financial advice, health care advice, or psychiatric care. Consult a qualified professional before you make a decision that could get you into trouble.

jessesmithbooks.com • tomispress.com

Hardcover ISBN 978-1-958337-08-0
Paperback ISBN 978-1-958337-26-4
E-book ISBN 978-1-958337-27-1

Library of Congress Control Number: 2024910184

First printing: Sept. 24, 2024. Second printing: Nov. 15, 2024.

Several brief portions of this text were first published to the author's blog or social media accounts from 2021 to 2023.

This text contains an excerpt from "The Power of Purpose" by Jesse S. Smith, which was first published to the Motivation Champs website in 2023, courtesy of Dominick Domasky.

The poem "Intrusive Thoughts" ©2021 was first published by Tomis Press in the collection *A Year Outside of Time* under the pen name, Titus Naso. Used by permission.

Self-help / Motivational / Spirituality

Part 1: Introduction

1.1 First, Let's Talk About You

You are here to do amazing things with your life. The key to unlocking your potential is to get started. Whatever you're facing, whatever you hope to accomplish, whatever you dream of doing or becoming, you can start today.

You can begin by accepting yourself as you are right now: because deep in your soul, **you are an awesome person**.

If that statement causes you discomfort or makes you feel like arguing, then this book really is meant for you. You can learn to love yourself.

Wherever you are in life, you can set yourself on the path to being happier and more successful. You can choose to improve your daily experience, to live the kind of life that makes you feel happy and fulfilled. You can choose to improve your circumstances. Whatever your dreams, you can achieve amazing things with your life: and you can start today.

You can overcome difficulties. You can overcome setbacks. You can overcome all the meaningless shit that life throws in your path, because life throws that shit at everyone.

You can have a better day tomorrow. You can take steps to have a better future. You can become a better version of yourself. You can make that choice. You can take these steps simply by **deciding that's who you truly are**.

It's time to begin working on a new project: the project of making your life amazing. I believe you can do it. Discover the possibilities and enjoy the journey!

Start today.

1.2 This is Me

Hi, my name is Jesse, it's nice to meet you.

I'm basically just a regular guy. I am not a doctor, or a psychologist, or any sort of celebrity. I have a business background and a number of projects in the works, but as I write this I'm a humble stay-at-home Dad. That's not what qualifies me to write this book.

Instead, my primary qualification for writing this book is that **I have been down in the shit**.

Yes, my friends, I have been down in it; and I have returned from that experience to lead a more meaningful, more joyful life afterwards. That's what I'm here to talk about.

So if you are presently down in it yourself, I hope that some of these lessons learned will help you find your way back.

Regardless of where you are in life: as you strive to get more out of life and simultaneously give back more to the people you love, I believe the same ideas that helped me return from my own personal rock bottom can offer you practical guidance for daily life, rooted in familiar concepts and ancient wisdom.

That's my value proposition. That's what I hope to offer you here.

I found my way to self-help the way many people find their way to religion: it shone a bright light for me when I was at a dark place in my life.

Yes, my friends, I struggled with the clinical depression and anxiety of my own personal rock bottom for *five* desolate years following a business failure. I felt truly hopeless.

Then I found hope.

And after I found hope, I went on to experience life as an amazing adventure once more.

Since then, I have campaigned for public office, worked on a movie production, traveled abroad, ran my first half-marathon, and taken my kids camping. I have released a new album of music, and even self-published several volumes of poetry under a pen name.

Once you begin to believe that anything is possible, then you become unstoppable.

Campaigning for public office in particular was a life-changing experience. I walked up and down the back streets of this district, knocking on doors and talking to voters. In many ways the experience reinforced my core belief that most people are basically decent, and we humans really have a lot in common with one another, despite the various differences that tend to feel so significant.

I invite you to consider the implications of this personal experience.

I found my way to the philosophy of self-help in 2019, when I was at my worst: depressed, hopeless, and bitter.

Just three years later, I was a major party candidate for the State legislature in the 2022 general election.

It was a dramatic life turnaround.

What changed?

And more importantly, **how can my experience help you?**

Well, let's be clear about this, right up front: it wasn't easy. The change in my life did not happen overnight. I did not simply manifest it with my thoughts. This is real life, not a movie. In real life, you don't get to squeeze all the hard work of personal transformation into a three-minute training montage. It has taken years. It has taken sweat, hard work, and some difficult conversations.

And let's be clear: some of the work is still ongoing; and some of the work will continue for the rest of my life.

But whatever I did, you could do, too. It's within your grasp.

Yes, you.

If I could do this, then you can do it, too! I believe that you can.

You don't have to run for public office, if that's not your thing. You don't have to start jogging, if that's not your thing. You don't have to start a business, if that's not your thing. You don't have to write a book, if that's not your thing. You don't have to teach overseas, if that's not your thing. But **you can do any of these things, if you choose to!** What's "your thing" might change over time; and that's okay, too.

Whatever you're into, whoever you dream of being, you can choose to live that life and be that person.

It's an amazing and powerful freedom, when you learn to see it. There is no limit to what you can achieve, if you choose to.

If you have some audacious life goal, pursue it! In ten or twenty years you may define "success" differently from how you picture it now; and yet, success can be yours. Or, if you just want to live in a state of contentment where you are now: you can do that too, if you choose to.

You can start today.

1.3 This is Self-Help

You have the power to improve your life!

Even if your circumstances are difficult to change, you have the power to improve your response to difficulties. And when you succeed in improving your habitual responses, I believe you will find that your experience of life will improve, as well.

If you are really, really unhappy with your life right now, then changing yourself probably sounds like a welcome relief. You might be grateful to hear Benjamin Hardy's message that *Personality Isn't Permanent.*

However, I find that people who are *not* at rock bottom tend to express skepticism about this idea. So if it helps, please feel welcome to look at it this way:

It's more about **finding your true self**, rather than changing yourself into someone else.

You don't have to become someone else. That's not the idea. Instead, you can choose to be your own best self. It's about being **the best version of you**, the real you, the *you* that the world deserves to see. Because there is a person inside of you who's trying to shine.

What do you want? It's a simple question, but it's surprisingly difficult to answer.

Often, we reflexively reply that we want another person to do something different. We think, "All my problems would be solved if someone else would just something-or-other." But we cannot change other people; and our attempts to compel others to change often end up driving conflict, frustration, and disappointment in our lives. As decent humans, we must neither force nor manipulate others into doing what we want them to do: for that is not the true path. Instead, we must learn to state, clearly and concisely, what we want for ourselves.

What is your dream? What is your purpose? Who do you see when you picture your ideal self?

If you cannot answer this yet, that's okay! Thinking about it at length will be an important step in your personal journey. Brainstorm a bit. Give yourself permission to consider many possibilities, wild adventurous possibilities, dreams that may have seemed so unrealistic in the past that you haven't allowed yourself to say them out loud. It's time. Go ahead and say it! And then give yourself permission to discard other possibilities that don't currently fit into your larger plan: even if those other possibilities are quite appealing, or even if you've already put quite a bit of work into them. If it's important enough, you can return to it later. Right now, prioritize.

Do more of what you love. When you are so engaged with your work that you have trouble tearing yourself away from your state of "flow," then you know you are in a good line of work. Try to be that engaged in every area of your life: personal, spiritual, recreational, and professional.

Identify what you want in life. Focus on what you want. And tell other people what you want! You're much more likely to achieve your goals if you're able to state them clearly.

Figure out the steps that will get you started on your journey from here to there, and go for it. Don't quietly tolerate a life that makes you miserable. Set goals. Set boundaries. Care for yourself first, that you may effectively care for others. Be assertive, but do it in a way that is strategic. Form alliances. Live your purpose.

Your concept of your own "purpose" may change over time; or it may not. What's important is that your current life's work is in alignment with your sense of purpose.

And yes, there are times in life when we all must perform drudgery, unpleasant or repetitive tasks, or menial labor: because that work must be done, and it falls on us to get it done. It's often difficult to feel fulfilled, or "living in line with our purpose," when we are performing work of this type. Yet although nobody really *enjoys* such work, even the performance of it can be a part of the larger picture of fulfilling your purpose in life. This is why Thich Nhat Hanh encourages us to practice mindfulness while washing the dishes, that we might live each moment more fully.

So try to learn to see the larger picture; and remember to be grateful that, for example, by doing what you're doing now, you're able to live the life you want and support those you love. And if the work you're doing isn't meeting your basic needs, then now is a good time to figure out a path to a better and more fulfilling line of work for you.

Start today.

1.3.1 It Has Been Said Before

There is little in this book that could be described as "new." On the contrary! This book repeatedly references not just other self-help authors, but also the wisdom of the world's ancient religions: including Judeo-Christianity, Buddhism, and Taoism. I would argue that self-help and self-improvement are closely related to the religious experience. You say "born again," I say "personal transformation." In many ways, it's the same thing. As Lao Tzu observes in the *Tao Te Ching*,

> "Why does everyone love the Tao so much?
>   Isn't it because you find what you seek, and are forgiven when you sin?

Therefore, this is the greatest treasure in the universe."[1]

Thus I would argue that major world religions and the modern self-help movement are very closely related. Each offers a path to the sort of transcendent experience that gives life new meaning and purpose.

Reading a motivational book is about finding inspiration. It's not just dry data. A self-help book offers an experience. If you repeat the experience often enough (for example, by reading or listening to lots of self-help books), you may at last succeed in **changing the story you tell yourself about your life**: and that's the key to personal transformation.

Changing your internal narrative is the core, the foundation, the cornerstone of your personal transformation program. It's arguably the most important piece of the puzzle. This is what we're here to do.

Your mindset shift is the key to turning your life around. If your life has been headed in the wrong direction for a long time, and you're ready for your life to change, then you're going to have to begin to change the way you think

---

1 *Tao Te Ching*, Chapter 62. I favor the translation by Gia-fu Feng and Jane English.

about things. Be prepared to return to tackle this again and again, because longstanding patterns do not change overnight.

Of course, a mindset shift is not *sufficient* all by itself. You also have to do the work!

But I'm here to tell you from experience that doing the work is not sufficient all by itself, either. You can work and work and work; but if your work is not properly focused, you may spin your wheels, waste your efforts, and exhaust yourself getting nowhere.

You have to **reprogram your mind**. In its most basic form, that's what this is all about. You have to change your habitual mental defaults. That takes a lot of conscious effort. In order to achieve successful change, you are going to need frequent reminders. That's why it helps to completely immerse yourself in self-help ideas for a while, as you go through your own transformation process. You may enjoy a variety of podcasts, YouTube videos, and guided meditation apps, as well as self-help books, many of which are available as audio books. Allow yourself to explore; and allow yourself the freedom to choose not to finish any particular resource that doesn't speak to your concerns. (If it's important enough, you can always come back to it later.) Focus on the content that makes your awareness vibrate at a higher frequency, in a manner of speaking. In other words, pursue your interests.

How much a particular book (or other resource) resonates with you at a given time depends in part on where you are in your life when you read (or watch or listen to) it.

Self-help books are intended to give you inspiration and direction. Of course, it's up to you how you apply what you learn from them. Effective life change requires both internal work and also outward effort. You must ride the wave of inspiration to new heights, try new things in your life, and give it your all.

When we believe that change is possible, change becomes possible. But if we believe that nothing will ever improve, then our belief becomes a self-fulfilling prophecy. Therefore, we must focus our minds on possibilities, and on gratitude, in order to improve our outcomes.

The most important thing I've learned is that there is always hope. Never give up! You can rediscover your love for yourself. It is possible. You can rediscover your passion for life. You can rediscover your joy and your connection with the world.

Start today.

1.3.2: The Value of Faith

Believe in yourself.
Accept yourself for who you are.
Review all your past successes.
Be grateful for all that has gone well.
Have faith in yourself.

Believe that deep in your core is an energetic essence of *you* that's possessed of all the purity and goodness that any being of pure spirit can possess. Call it a soul, call it a divine presence, call it God if you prefer, call it Tao, call it Awareness, call it what you will. I don't care what you call it, but I ask you to take a chance, and allow yourself to believe that this inner vibration exists in a realm without sin or want, without regret or fear. You are perfect.

Believe that by focusing your conscious mind, you can become more at peace with yourself, improve your relationships with other people, and/or achieve more in life, depending on what you're trying to do at this stage in your life.

It's not for me to say what you want: you get to decide that for yourself. But for argument's sake, let's simplify it to its most basic level; and let's say that whatever it is you're trying to do right now, you're doing it because you want more happiness in life. That's good: now you have a goal.

Now, plant a seed of faith, and nourish it. The seed of faith you are planting is the belief that you can achieve your goal. You can change yourself, if you want to; you can change your life, if it needs changing.

But you must mind your mindset: because positive change is not going to happen if you tell yourself that change is impossible. If you tell yourself that it *won't* happen, then your negative belief becomes a self-fulfilling prophesy!

But if you stay positive, if you tell yourself, "This is going to happen!" and then you say it to yourself over and over again, "This is going to happen!" – by communicating this message of faith to your subconscious mind, you help ensure that **you will follow through**, invest the time and energy required, and take the necessary steps to make it happen. And when achieving your goal takes longer than you wanted, and it requires more effort than you'd hoped it would, and when you hit inevitable setbacks along the way, and you wonder if this really is even possible, or if it might be even worth all the trouble when you're so tired already: then that's when you look inwards at that faith you're nurturing inside yourself and you say, "**Yes**, dammit, this is going to be worthwhile, and I am going to do it. This is going to happen! Yes! I believe!"

This is the value of faith.

Faith keeps you going. It sustains your efforts. It makes you feel that your efforts are worthwhile.

Have faith in yourself.

1.4 Case Study: From Dropout to Doctor

I will tell you why I know for a fact that people can change their lives. I know this because I have seen it happen.

In fact, I know many amazing people, and I could tell a lot of inspiring stories about them. But right now, I want to start by telling you the story of one awesome person in particular.

This person is one of the most brilliant, amazing, strong, kind, and caring people you could ever hope to meet. Her name is Jessica.

Jessica tragically lost her father to a car accident when she was very young. After several years, her mother remarried; but Jessica had a difficult relationship with her new stepfather.

As a teenager, Jessica left home and moved out on her own.

She also dropped out of high school.

She never finished high school. During the next few years, she attempted to take some classes at community college; but given her unstable life situation, she had trouble focusing on academic pursuits, and ended up with several failed classes on her transcripts.

She worked unskilled minimum wage positions. She lived in a shared apartment that was so overcrowded, there were people sleeping not just on the couch but even in the closet.

She got married at a young age. They lived with her in-laws in a mobile home trailer for a while. She got divorced a few years later.

Many of us, finding ourselves in such a situation, would have looked at this life and accepted it as our destiny. But not Jessica.

When she was in her late twenties, Jessica decided that she wanted to do something meaningful with her life.

She didn't know at first what she wanted to do; but she knew that her current situation was not an acceptable end point for her life. She wanted to do more. So she set to work turning her life around.

First, she went back to the local community college and got her GED. She was starting from a position of negative credits, due to the earlier failed attempt that had left a stain on her transcript. But it had been several years since then, and she was prepared to try again. She took those classes over again, and she worked her ass off, and she succeeded.

Then she transferred to a nearby university, and completed the coursework she needed to earn her undergraduate degree.

During this time, she had a major revelation. Once the idea occurred, she knew it was the answer she had been seeking. She wanted to become a physician. Once she had decided on this goal, nothing was going to stand in her way.

This was not an easy journey for Jessica. She struggled along the way, and borrowed staggering sums of money in student loans. There was turmoil in her personal life. Meanwhile, although by now she had earned her undergraduate degree, it had not been a degree with a pre-med focus; so she was compelled to go back to university for those prerequisite courses, just so she could even *apply* to medical school. And even once all this was done, due to various disappointments and mix-ups, her entrance to medical school had to be postponed for another year.

It was a long, slow process; but she persevered, and in the end she succeeded, and began her studies in medical school.

Of course, medical school itself was extraordinarily challenging. Many of her classmates dropped out or failed out in the first year. These were people accustomed to being the best and the brightest: and they discovered that simply being intelligent is not enough. You have to persevere. And that's what Jessica did. She persisted.

Partway through medical school, Jessica got married again, started a family, and took a year off from school to care for her infant while her husband worked a desk job at a print shop.

After Jessica graduated from medical school, she and her family moved to a new city for her three-year residency program.

Medical residency was a special kind of sleepless living Hell. Physicians who have just finished school but aren't yet certified to practice are required to essentially live in the hospital where they work. There are even bunk beds in the staff lounge; not that the residents ever had time to sleep more than a few minutes before alarms went off and sent them scurrying to the next emergency. It was physically and emotionally exhausting. Some of the other residents dropped out because the program was too stressful. These were people who had already completed medical school, who decided not to get licensed as doctors rather than undergo the grueling requirements of medical residency. But Jessica powered through. Even so, residency kept her away from her family, and when she did come home all she wanted to do was sleep.

At last, after completing the grueling residency program, Jessica got a job as a physician at a family practice clinic, and began to work in her new profession.

And that's how a high school dropout went on to become a doctor.

That's perhaps the most tremendous life turnaround I could hope to describe to you.

Her life change did not happen overnight. It was quite the opposite. Jessica's journey to turn her life around had taken her a decade. Along the way, she had worked harder than she'd ever imagined possible, faced her fears, overcome obstacles, and triumphed.

Today Jessica has been practicing at the same clinic for over a decade. She is well-loved by her patients, respected by her colleagues, and a valuable member of her community. She has delivered babies, she has alleviated chronic health problems, she has eased the suffering of the terminally ill, and she has helped to improve the well-being of the people in her community.

Her patients love her so much that some drive long distances to continue visiting her even after they have moved away. She gives back to the world through her work, all day, every day, and she makes the world a better place.

The reason I know this story so well, is because this amazing woman is my wife.[2] At the time of this book's publication, we have been married for more than 18 years, and we have two adorable children. I am proud to be part of her life.

Jessica is the perfect example of someone who fought hard and struggled, overcame obstacles, and at long last achieved great things with her life.

So if you are faced with what seems like a difficulty you can't get past, just remember Jessica. She did it, and so can you.

The lesson of Jessica's life is that with hard work and determination, we really can overcome any obstacle, no matter how insurmountable it may seem.

The secret to Jessica's success is that she had a goal.

---

2   Yes, my name is Jesse and my wife's name is Jessica. Yes, our names are very similar. No, you are not the first person to notice this. No, our parents did not plan that, ewww.

Once she had identified her goal, it became the one thing that she wanted more than anything else; and she focused her mind, her body and soul, and every aspect of her entire life, on the attainment of that goal. She **decided** that she wanted to be a physician; and once she had decided that, nothing was going to stop her. In the midst of financial difficulties and personal upheavals, she persevered, she persisted, she kept striving. She knew what she wanted, and she went for it. It was hard, and it took many long years, and she was the oldest person in her graduating class at medical school: but once she knew what she wanted, she was unstoppable.

You can be like Jessica. You can be unstoppable. It's not easy, but you can do it. I have confidence in you. It begins with mindset, and that's what we're going to work on in this book.

Let's get started!

Part 2: Be Good to Yourself

Before we go any farther, I'd like to propose two basic ground rules for this discussion, and I'll attempt to hold myself to them throughout the text.

We're not here to compare traumas. Sadly, all too often people tend to believe that their own trauma "doesn't count" for some reason. We have all heard such disturbing horror stories of what someone else went through that we may begin to downplay the significance of our own experiences. In your life, you may have already encountered the sort of assholes[3] who will tell you outright that "someone else lived through something worse,

---

3 I generally discourage name-calling, so I feel guilty for this lapse, so I would like to propose that in this book the term "asshole" is specific to a particular **mindset**: *not* to particular individuals. We have all been assholes at some time in our lives. We do not have to remain assholes forever. No one does. People are redeemable.

so why are you complaining?" Don't fall for that shit. Nobody else's experience is a reflection on your experience. If you're in pain, that's all we need to know at this point. Your experience is valid.

We're not here to judge. There is no blame here. What happened in the past is in the past. It doesn't matter whose fault it was. You might believe that it was your fault, or someone else's fault, or society's fault: but we don't care about that right now. Leave blame behind. Instead, we are taking responsibility for our own lives, starting with this moment. Right now, we're going to take responsibility for turning things around and making the best of things henceforth. That's it. How we got to this point is irrelevant. Our work at this time is to resolve the current situation as best we can, and move on from here. In other words, we're just here to deal with the mess. Get ready to get your hands dirty!

That's it! This is not, primarily, a book of rules. It is more like a book of suggestions.

Here are a few more suggestions.

Life is a game. Have fun: that's more important than we sometimes remember.

There are many things that connect us as humans; so we should try to enjoy each other's company, and to help each other when we can.

And you know, we're all still learning.

In *Meditation for Fidgety Skeptics*, Dan Harris shares the insight that even Buddhist monks who have spent a lifetime meditating still sometimes find their minds wandering during meditation. We get better with practice; but perfection is illusory. You might attain something close to perfection, briefly; but you can't expect it to last. It's true for Buddhist monks, it's true for me, and it's true for you, too. So whatever it is you're doing in life, keep practicing! And don't beat yourself up if you aren't perfect. In fact, **nobody is perfect**.

Perfection should not be the goal, much less the expectation.

The practice is the path.

The goal is to strut your funky stuff.

Beyond that, while there are lots of folks who like to quibble, I still believe the Golden Rule is a reasonable starting point on our journey to a better life:

"Do unto others as you would have them do unto you."[4]

And if you think about that well-worn injunction, it still has some surprisingly relevant implications for us.

For the purpose of beginning your self-help journey, consider the implications if the reverse of this Biblical aphorism is also true.

In other words, consider that if we're going to practice this:

"Do unto others as you would have others do unto you."

then we must also practice this:

"Do unto *yourself* as you would have *others* do unto *anyone*."

In other words, you should treat yourself with the same basic fundamental human dignity that we all must be expected to extend to our neighbors and colleagues and friends and family and community members.

---

4   Based on Luke 6:31, "And as ye would that men should do to you, do ye also to them likewise."

That sounds so basic, doesn't it? And yet, how often do we find ourselves breaking this simple rule? How often do we find that we are abusing ourselves? Talking shit about ourselves? We allow our bad habits to continue, because that's easier than doing the work to transform our lives. We speak ill of ourselves, we eat poorly, we sleep poorly, we expend our mental energy on conflict and uncharitable thoughts. We know we should improve our own physical and mental health, but we...

wait a minute, we *are* doing something about it! We are doing something right now: you are, and so am I. I'm writing this book, and you're reading it. We are both actively trying to break the cycle, right now. Right here in this very moment, **we're making a change**. So instead of lamenting the past, let's give ourselves some credit for what we're doing in the present. This is progress! You're awesome, reader, and don't ever forget it.

So keep doing that.

Love yourself.

2.0.1: "The Flipper Factor"

You hear a lot of advice.

Sometimes advice is helpful; but sometimes it is extremely unhelpful. Much so-called "advice" is demeaning, or even authoritarian. It's up to you to choose which advice you listen to; and it's up to you to maintain firm boundaries in the face of unhelpful advice and the sort of people who insist on offering it to you unasked.

Even the best of good advice is not law. Advice is situational. The same advice does not apply in all circumstances.

For example, if you're going scuba diving for the first time, your instructor would do well to advise you to wear an air tank and flippers; but if you're going skydiving for the first time, then a parachute is a more appropriate tool.

You don't want your skydiving instructor to hand you a pair of flippers after you have jumped out of an airplane.

I call this "The Flipper Factor."

Flippers are useful if you're scuba diving; but flippers are an unnecessary encumbrance if you're skydiving.[5]

---

5 And if you're jumping out of an airplane and skydiving straight into the ocean so you can scuba dive into a supervillain's secret lair… then the point remains: advice is situational.

Advice is situational.

2.1 You Can Only Change Yourself

Everybody wants to change the world.

And most of us would like the people around us to change.

Few of us are prepared to change ourselves.

But as it turns out, you are the only person you have power over.

That's why one of the most important of all self-help principles is the idea that you can only change yourself. You cannot change other people.

Often, we wish other people would change. There's a lot we don't like about other people, so we think they should change themselves to better suit us.

As nice as that may sound on some days, we know that the world doesn't really work like that.

You can only change yourself.

No, you can't make other people change; and speaking rudely to them is *particularly* unlikely to make anyone change in the way we think they should change. On the other hand, remaining polite regardless of the situation can sometimes salvage relationships.

Sometimes we may even read a self-help book, and we think to ourselves, "I really wish so-and-so would read this book, it might help them to fix their personal issues or whatever is wrong with them." That's missing the point. We can't change other people; and we wouldn't really want to take on that awesome responsibility even if we could.

If you try to force others to conform to your expectations, it will only make them hate you. Now, unfortunately, there are times when picking up a couple of random haters here and there is unavoidable. (In the social media era, attracting haters is not a bug: it's a feature.) But as Machiavelli reminds us, we should avoid being hated, if at all possible.

Therefore, constantly venting our irritation and resentment on everyone around us, in the misguided belief that doing so will somehow magically make the whole world conform to every single one of our lengthy list of unreasonable expectations, is a bad habit that we *all* need to break.

Instead, we need to intentionally focus our attention on what is good. We need to intentionally focus our minds on feeling grateful for all the good things in our lives, in each moment, especially in this moment, now.

This is how you can begin to change yourself.

You can change how you respond.

You can change how you react to difficult people and situations. You can change whether or not you get upset when you are frustrated. That is within your power. And you may find that changing the way you react to frustration improves your enjoyment of life overall. You may even sometimes find that changing your reactions to other people makes them more willing to compromise with you or even accommodate your requirements.

You can change how you interpret things. Yes, you can look at *anything* from a different perspective: casual remarks, significant events in your past, all of it. Some asshole tried to hurt your feelings with an insult? How small they must feel inside, to lash out at the world in such an immature way. You experienced a serious trauma? You proved that you can fuckin' *survive* that shit, because **you are strong**, and don't you ever forget it.

You can only change yourself: but, and this is a key caveat, if you make the effort, you just might find that when you decide to change yourself, other people choose to change, as well.

Sometimes, you'll find that when you're nicer to other people, other people are nicer to you. Not always! But sometimes.

Sometimes, if you smile at someone they will smile back at you. Not always! There are a lot of grumpy people out there. But sometimes a simple smile can brighten someone's day, so give it a try. Making these small connections is rewarding on a deeper level than we tend to realize.

If you're a parent, then sometimes you'll find that when you get better sleep and avoid snapping at your kids, then your kids are better behaved and exhibit fewer behaviors that require reprimands. Not always! But it makes a difference.

In my own life, I believe that my regular running practice probably provided an example for one of my neighbors, who started running as well; and I'm *certain* (because they told me so) that my efforts in campaigning for political office helped to inspire two other individuals in my extended social circle to run for their own respective offices locally – and one of them won! I consider that a **major win** right there. Even if I didn't get into office myself, I helped to inspire someone who successfully got elected to local office (on the Library board, in this case).

So remember, we influence the people around us – and they influence us in turn.

And if you think about it, you already influence the people in your life: perhaps directly, or perhaps in subtle ways. That influence matters, and you can use your influence to do good in the world.

You make a difference.

2.2: Love Yourself

There is no "first rule" of self-help.

Regardless of which rule comes first, I believe the most important rule of self-help is to **love yourself**. Only when you love yourself can you love others from a position of strength.

Everyone is worthy of love. Everyone is worthy of being treated with compassion, dignity, and respect. And "everyone" includes you. You are worthy of love. You are worthy of being treated with compassion, dignity, and respect. And you are worthy of changing your life.

Amazingly, when we treat others with love, we become more worthy of love.

When we feel insecure, or when we are angry, or when we are filled with negativity and cynicism: then we are unable to fully share the best part of ourselves with the world. Only after rediscovering some sort of inner connection are we better able to connect with others.

That's why the most common recurring analogy in self-help is the iconic image of the oxygen mask on the airplane. If you've ever flown on a commercial airliner, you may recall the safety briefing at the beginning of the flight, when the flight attendant instructed you: "In the event of a loss of cabin pressure, oxygen masks will drop from the overhead compartment. Be sure to put on your own oxygen mask before assisting other passengers." If you don't see to your own needs first, you might not be able to effectively help the other passenger before you pass out. Those around you may not be able to give you the assistance you need: so if you were to help others without first taking care of yourself, then you could fatally exhaust your own reserves, and die. Instead, you must ensure your own well-being before assisting other passengers. That way, you can help them from a position of strength.

Or, as my friend Diana Usher said recently, your own bucket has to be full before you can pour into someone else's.

We all want to be the strong. We want to be seen as generous and helpful and loving and giving. But we can't be seen this way by everyone all the time: because eventually, someone will ask us for something that we're not prepared to give. Therefore, part of loving yourself is enforcing boundaries to protect yourself from the sometimes unreasonable demands of the world.

If you want to make the world a better place, begin by loving yourself.

2.2.1 You Are Worthy of Love

It's almost embarrassing to hear someone say that, isn't it? But it's true: you are worthy of love! As a human being you have dignity, potential, and inherent worth.

The mind tends to rebel against such statements, especially when we are new to this process. Engaging in a bit of projection here, I'm going to give voice to some of the objections that your mind might possibly raise at this time.

"Whaddya mean, I'm worthy of love?" argues the mind. "You don't even know me!"

You're a human being; and as a human being, you are worthy of love.

"But everybody hates me!"

That's a rather extreme statement. I doubt it's true. Even if a few people have made their negative sentiments painfully clear, they don't represent *everybody*! There have been times when some people have accepted and even loved you. Remember that. Look for the bright spots, figure out what was different about those better times, and do more of that. You have potential, and you are worthy of love.

"You're trying to tell me that I have potential? But... what if I were dying of cancer right now?"

Every moment of every day is a blessing and I hope you will make the most of it. If you're literally on your deathbed and in your final moments right now, then I wish you the most painless passing possible, and the best equanimity you can find, and closure with your loved ones, and joyful reflections on the life you have lived. That said, chances are you're probably not reading this book on your deathbed right now.

"You're right, I'm not reading this book on my deathbed. How did you guess?"

The book is called *Start Today*. It's not a very deathbed sort of book. It's the opposite. It's a book for people who want to **start living**.

"Anyway," the mind returns to the subject at hand, "the point here is that I'm unworthy of love! So-and-so told me so!"

I'm sorry for whatever you went through, and for all the people who have hurt you. But you don't have to believe all the hurtful things they said to you. You can let that go, and love yourself, because you are worthy of love.

"All my life!" complains the mind. "This person, and that person, and some other person!"

When we've been hurt, we tend to get into negative patterns, and those negative patterns tend to repeat, in ways small and large, throughout our lives. We provoke, and we get provoked. We instinctively seek out people who remind us of those who have evoked a strong emotional response from us in the past; and just like those people from our past, the people we seek out end up hurting us or provoking us. Some of that's them, and sometimes some of it's us; and trying to figure out who to blame just winds up leading down the road to hate, so let's not go there. We're not here to hate anyone. We're here to love ourselves; and as part of loving ourselves, we're re-learning to love others, as well.

"But, you don't understand!" says the mind. "I did something bad! That's why I'm unworthy of love!"

There is no judgment more powerful than self-judgment; and there is no emotion more toxic than shame.

That's why Aldous Huxley once wrote:

"Chronic remorse is a most undesirable sentiment. If you have behaved badly, repent, make what amends you can, and address yourself to the task of behaving better next time. On no account brood over your wrongdoing. Rolling in the muck is not the best way of getting clean."[6]

Words of wisdom right there.

Everyone makes mistakes. The more time we spend feeling bad about our mistakes, the more likely we are to do something *else* bad. As Huxley said, it's much better to make amends if you can, and move on.

It's even better yet to try to figure out how to treat your past mistake as a **learning experience**. Can you do something differently in the future, to avoid experiencing this sort of thing again?

---

6 From Huxley's Foreword to the 1946 reprint edition of his classic dystopian sci-fi novel, *Brave New World*, in the context of apologizing for what might be characterized as plot holes in the story. Very slightly edited for clarity.

Whatever it was, your mistake, series of misjudgments, or other bad habits: it may seem insurmountable to you right now; but if you are able to step back and look at it from a larger perspective, I hope you will see that it's not really that bad.

It's not that bad. It's not that important. It's in the past. It's done. I forgive you. Forgive yourself. You don't have to feel bad about it any more.

"But how can you say that?" asks the defiant mind.

I can say that, first of all because I feel pretty confident in asserting that most of the sort of people who turn to a book like this after hitting rock bottom in their personal lives have never committed any sort of a violent crime; and furthermore, generally speaking, the sort of people who *do* turn to violent crime are often uninterested in reading books of any kind, unfortunately.

That said, no matter what you have done, believe in the power of redemption. You can choose to be a better person tomorrow than the person you were yesterday.

Practice awareness. Learn to disregard negative judgments of yourself and other people.

Focus on the good. Choose the good. Be the good.

Mistakes are learning experiences.

The past does not have to predict the future. Life can change.

You can change.

2.2.1.1   Case Study: How Do You Define Greatness?

Too often, we spend so much time beating ourselves up over our past mistakes that we forget to give ourselves credit for our past successes. You have wins in your past and present, on some level, and those are worth celebrating. Don't be held back by the way other people measure success.

In our culture we tend to try to define "greatness" numerically. We tend to believe that our "importance" in the world can be measured by our salary, or by the value of our house, or by the number of followers we have on social media, or by the number of sales our book or album or whatever has enjoyed, or whether or not we can afford to buy status symbols like luxury cars.

But these are gross approximations at best; and as measures of greatness they often fall far short of accuracy.

For an obvious example, many social media followers are "bots" – accounts run by automated software programs whose sole purpose is to make somebody look artificially important (or to harass someone who the programmer wants to feel *unimportant*). Sure, you may have a lot of so-called "followers," but they're not even human beings! Where's the value in that? Isn't connecting with people supposed to be the whole point?

But connection and relationships are intangible and often fleeting. Follower counts are a status symbol, but they are not an accurate measure of interpersonal relationships. Interpersonal connection and human relationships cannot be accurately quantified like the numbers on a corporate balance sheet. They can only be felt in the moment.

In exactly the same way, I believe that true greatness cannot be measured: it can only be felt in the moment.

For example, there once was a band named Deep Banana Blackout. I was a fan. I would go so far as to describe them as the most noteworthy up-and-coming act on the scene at around the turn of the millennium.

Deep Banana Blackout were a funky blues-rock jam band with a horn section and a female lead singer like the reincarnation of Janis Joplin. They put on an incredible live show. They had a small but devoted following on the East Coast: fans who knew the words to their songs and would sing along while the band played.

The band released a studio album, and followed it up with a double-CD live album, which they sold from a merchandise table at their rockin' shows. I caught them at Mt. Tabor Theater in Portland on a friend's recommendation, and I was absolutely blown away by their stellar performance. A year or two later, they headlined at the Oregon Country Fair. They seemed to really be going places.

But the band's drummer and singer were married; and then, they got divorced: and that was the end of the band.

Deep Banana Blackout never became a well-known household name. They never had a "top 40" hit single or a hot-selling album. Most people have never heard of them. And yet, two decades after they broke up, I still enjoy listening to their music, especially the live album. They wrote some really quality material, every bit as good as our favorite classic rock songs or jazz standards. The band put on impeccable performances of technically complex musical passages, and they brought an unstoppable energy to their shows that made the crowds go wild.

That to me is true greatness. It's not about how many people know your name. It's about being awesome in the way that only you can be awesome, and connecting with the special few who can appreciate you on that level.

So don't be held back by other people's measurement of "greatness" or "success." You have already achieved much, and there is greatness in your future.

2.2.2 Speak Well of Yourself

For most of my life, I held the mistaken belief that saying bad things about myself was an amusing and socially acceptable sign of humility. In the time and the subculture of my coming of age, self-deprecating humor seemed to be in vogue. In other words, I grew up believing that talking shit about oneself was funny, and even kind of expected. So throughout my life I have often said things like, "Oh, I'm not good at that; oh, and I'm terrible at that, too; no, I'm not talented, I'm just an idiot; I'm not good at anything, everything I do is a mistake, ha ha."

Perhaps you have similar bad habits: and let's be clear, this is a *very* bad habit. This dynamic can cause lasting harm: because our own minds may tend to take these little self-deprecating remarks a little too literally. Although we tell ourselves that "it's just a joke," even so we begin to really deeply believe these awful things that we say about ourselves. These types of negative self-beliefs can become the greatest limiting factor in our own lives. So throw off the shackles of negative self-talk, and experience the limitlessness of positivity!

Worse yet, other people believe the negative things we say about ourselves. They take it literally. My experience has been that the "humorous negative self-talk" model of humility utterly fails in its intended purpose of making us more likable and relatable to others. Instead, when we talk about ourselves in this way, others tend to shower us with contempt.

I can only speak from my own personal experience. My experience (which it took me far too long to recognize and analyze properly) has been that when I have said negative things about myself to others, they did not see this as "humility." They simply took my self-deprecating remarks at face value. Some people took this as a sign that they should avoid my company. Others mocked me to my face. And even some of my closest friends sometimes stored up these self-deprecating remarks of mine, and used them as ammunition against me later on: to try to bring me down a notch; or to prevent me from moving up, or moving on. Then I would get angry at them, because with my low self-esteem issues, the last thing I needed was other people tearing me down. And yet, in a way, I had brought this upon myself by saying these things about myself in the first place. From their perspective, I had set the standard by *insulting myself first*.

Well, I can't change other people; but I can change myself.

I can't force others to speak respectfully about me; but I can choose to speak respectfully about myself.

And if I do speak about myself in respectful terms, then this will influence some (but not all!) of the people around me to speak to me, and about me, in more respectful terms.

So don't say bad things about yourself.

For myself, instead of sharing stories about my own failings in a doomed attempt to connect with other people through the idea that "we all make mistakes," it's better for me to keep my own mistakes reasonably private, treat them as learning experiences, and instead try to present a more polished, professional, accomplished, confident, successful image to the world. This may be a winning strategy for you, as well.

Give yourself the respect you deserve. When people see you respecting yourself, they are more likely to respect you, too. And no, this is not a universal law: it is just a general tendency. But the great thing about noticing tendencies is, if you can get a whole bunch of general tendencies on your side, then you tend to be more successful in all of your efforts.

May all your efforts succeed.

2.3 Forgive Yourself

Let's face it: if things have gone wrong in your life, then you have probably made some bad decisions at some point along the way.

But it's not just you. We all have. There's no point being ashamed of this. Everyone has made a bad decision at some point.

It is just as narcissistic to say, "Everything is my fault" as it is to say, "Nothing is my fault." Neither of these statements is true! The truth is more complicated than that. Reality is an intricate web of subtlety and nuance which is not easily described by slogans and pithy catchphrases.

Liberate yourself from judgmental dogmas. Free your mind from hate and blame and guilt: both your own, and that of others. The only true path to peace must be found through acceptance and forgiveness. Accept yourself. Forgive yourself. Accept others. Forgive others.

Avoid value judgments and name-calling. Few people are completely "bad," and even fewer people are completely "good." We are all merely human.

You are human: and as a human, you deserve compassion, dignity, and respect.

Recognize your past mistakes without judging yourself; and allow this recognition to guide better choices in the future.

Your past mistakes are not a reflection of your present character. Your past mistakes are simply information that you can use to help guide you towards better decisions in the future. Your past is a learning experience. Your past has brought you to this place, and from this place you get to choose a brighter path forward.

You are not your problems. You are not your diagnosis. You are not your mistakes. You are not the bad things that others have said to you or done to you in the past. You are not your bad thoughts about yourself.

We tend to identify with the problems in our lives, to bring them on board, to make them a part of ourselves, to carry them with us. We begin to believe that the problem is *who we are*. But you are so much more!

You are your hopes and dreams. You are your achievements: and if you think about it, there are many! You are your core values, and you are the actions you take to live those values, here and now. You are the energetic being who observes and understands, and who is capable of letting go of all judgment: even judgment of self. You are the efforts you make to overcome the obstacles in your life. You are redeemed by your personal transformation. You are the kindness you show others. You are the service you perform on their behalf. You are the goodness you see in others. You are the beauty that you see in the world.

2.4 Believe in Yourself

The first thing you have to do, when you are ready to turn your life around, the first step you have to take, is to **believe you can do it**.

If you believe you can do it, then you will take steps to ensure that it will happen. You will overcome obstacles and setbacks, and eventually you will attain a new satisfaction from your life.

But if you don't believe that you can change your life, then you will not take the steps that make change possible. If you don't believe that you can change your life, then you won't. Instead of changing your life, you will just sit on your couch and stream low-budget movies to your television in the background while you use the Internet to snark at all those "arrogant narcissists" who are out there "thinking they're better than you" every day. It's probably all their fault that you can't do what you want to do with your life, right? **No.** None of that is right.

The fact is, you *can* change your life. You can decide to be a better person. You can choose to be more popular, more successful, more loving, more spiritual, more wealthy, more ethical, and more joyous. You can make that choice; and then you can make it happen. You can decide who you want to be: and then you can take steps to become that person. Where you end up in five years might not be exactly what you're envisioning here at the outset. But if you work at it, I believe that you will be able to accomplish more than you have ever dreamed, and feel an increased sense of satisfaction with your life.

The more you smile, the more you feel like smiling. The more you laugh, the more you feel like laughing. We tend to get more of what we focus on. So keep smiling! Laugh whenever you can. Focus on the good.

Believing in yourself can be really difficult when you're at rock bottom. That's why believing in yourself is so essential to your life transformation process.

I struggled with this. Following the failure of my business, I lost faith in myself. It was devastating. I wound up at rock bottom.

Building my confidence back required a lot of hard work; and it required me to learn to believe in myself once again. Eventually I found a sort of inner core of myself that I felt I could rely upon: an inner core of self that didn't squish under pressure, you might say. But first, I made myself jump through a whole lot of hoops, to prove to myself that I could believe in myself again; which is perhaps a rather silly way of going about this, as I'm sure many spiritual advisors and meditation gurus would tell you: but it's what worked for me. Different processes may be more or less effective for you. We're all wonderfully unique, so do whatever works best for your unique self, and do it with love. Most importantly, start today!

2.4.1 The importance of belief

If we want to improve our lives, we must believe that it's possible to improve our lives.

There's a well-known phenomenon in medicine known as the placebo effect. You have heard of this. When people believe they are taking some kind of miracle cure, it often makes them feel better: even when they are actually taking a sugar pill with no medical benefits whatsoever.

This concept is made beautifully relevant by the book *Chatter*, by Ethan Kross.

Kross and his associates conducted a study involving people who were suffering from a very painful physical condition known as Irritable Bowel Syndrome, or IBS. In the study, half of the participants were given a placebo. However, there was something different. Unlike double-blind pharmaceutical trials, in this study the participants who received the placebo were *told* that they would be receiving a placebo; and they received a briefing on the well-documented phenomenon of the placebo effect.

The study's results were remarkable. Check this out.

Even though they *knew* that the pill they had taken was a placebo, the people who took the placebo reported that they felt better afterwards!   Taking a placebo had alleviated the painful symptoms of their IBS.

This is a truly amazing finding!   It demonstrates that the mind has tremendous power over our physical well-being and the circumstances of our lives. The key is that we must believe in this power, in order for it to work.

This phenomenon can help to explain the miracle cures attributed to faith healers, saints, and prophets throughout human history. The power of belief itself has such healing power that it has provided the founding mythology for major world religions. As Kross points out in his book, people who believe in New Age mystical phenomena such as magnets, or reiki, or crystals, or essential oils, or whatever: these people actually feel better as a result of their engagement with these practices.   But that doesn't mean that the crystals themselves have some innate healing power, from any objectively scientific perspective: it means that *the mind* has innate healing powers, which are unlocked by the power of belief.

But that doesn't require us to have faith in falsehoods. As Kross and his colleagues demonstrated in their study, we can knowingly engage the power of our own mental circuitry, without relying on trickery. We can understand exactly what we are doing, and still obtain the benefits of the power of belief.

There's no cure-all. Change is a long, slow process.

But it's a process that you can start today.

2.4.2 Case Study: A Rock and Roll Icon's Moment of Self-Doubt

Everyone feels moments of self-doubt: even a rock and roll legend like Jimi Hendrix.

In the middle of one of the most iconic performances of his entire life, on the stage at Woodstock in the summer of 1969, Jimi Hendrix leaned in to the microphone and announced to the crowd, "You can leave if you want to, we're just jamming."

In that moment, one of the greatest guitar legends of all time had the same sense of humility and self-doubt as any of the rest of us. In that moment, Jimi Hendrix believed that the people in the audience might not want to bother listening to the remainder of the show, because the band was "just jamming."

And then he went on to deliver the highlights of **one of the best shows of his career**.

Everyone suffers from self-doubt and uncertainty sometimes. It's not just you. The key is to move on from that moment to your "Purple Haze" encore.

Move on from doubt by focusing on what you love, what you believe in, what you value, what you enjoy, and your expressions of who you are, who you want to be, and the kind of life you want to live.

You are meant to do something amazing.

Part 3: Be Good to Others

We all wish to be treated well; therefore, we all must do our best to treat others well.

3.1 Love People

Remember that all people are just people, everywhere and throughout time.

Some people look different, or act different, or believe different things, but we're still all just people.

Since we share a fundamental basic humanity with everyone, if we are to fully love ourselves, then on some level we must extend that love to all people, everywhere and throughout time: including people who look different, or act different, or believe different things from ourselves.

Of course we're going to disagree with them sometimes.

But it's really not necessary to battle them all the time.

Sometimes we can just be friends and neighbors and learn to get along.

That almost sounds controversial in our current sociopolitical environment. But this idea is not aligned with any particular party, movement, or ideology. It's a fundamental human principle. We can learn to get along.

The way I look at the Universe, everything is interconnected on some deeply mathematical level that most of us will never even begin to comprehend and that's okay. We, and all other people, and all of observable reality, are part of something larger than ourselves. That doesn't mean you can bend reality with your thoughts; or that distant planets affect your personality and fate; or whatever. It *does* mean that we really should extend the same love and compassion to other people that we would want them to extend to us: because on some deeper level, they are us, and we are all one.

Sorry if that's a bit too "woo."

The same basic idea is prevalent in Christianity, where Jesus admonishes us to, "Love thy neighbor as thyself." (Mark 12:31)

It's remarkably similar to the ancient wisdom of the *Tao Te Ching*, which says:

"Love the world as your own self; then you can truly care for all things."[7]

This concept is universal, transcending nationalities and borders and cultures and time itself.

Love others as you love yourself.

Doesn't matter who they are. Doesn't matter what they look like. Doesn't matter who they sleep with, so long as it's consensual. Doesn't matter if you enjoy their company. Doesn't even matter if they have hurt you in the past. We should still do our best to extend to them the basic love and respect due to all human beings.

That's hard sometimes; especially if we are bearing a grudge, or if we have gotten into a toxic relationship.

There has been a lot of chatter these past few years about "toxic people." Even my local grocery store has a book titled, *How to Deal With Toxic People* prominently displayed on its book rack. (Full disclosure, I have not read it.) In my view, all this talk of "toxic people" is no more than the **victim mentality** engaging in finger-pointing and blame. Perhaps we all do this at times; but when we recognize that we're

---

7   Chapter 13, as translated by Gia-fu Feng and Jane English.

falling into this toxic thought pattern, it's time to move on to healthier patterns.

When you find yourself blaming all your problems on "toxic people," or "narcissists," or your label of choice, whatever it may be: notice that you are indulging your victim mentality by engaging in blame and self-pity. It is often the case that, if you weren't so toxic to others, then they wouldn't be so toxic to you. Not always! But sometimes.

Yes, sometimes you meet a genuine "movie villain" – but probably not as often as you think.

More often, it's our *relationships* that sour. The other person has not changed, or not in the way we think. Instead, our relationship to them has changed. We stop caring for others as much as we used to.

Sometimes we accumulate small grievances and resentments until those grievances burst forth in an irrational venting of blame and shame, which cause lasting damage and make the other person wish to avoid us.

Sometimes we begin to associate an individual person with some negative incident or thought that has occurred, and then negativity infects every aspect of our future relationship with that person. Through the power of mental association, we get caught up in cycles where merely seeing this person makes us angry. The moment they walk into the room we are instantly prepared to begin arguing or even fighting. The moment we see them, we immediately adopt a rude tone, we speak sharply, we find fault, we lob accusations and generalizations for no reason. No wonder the other person responds in kind. Or perhaps you believe they always do it first? Perhaps; but even so, don't engage in tit-for-tat retaliation. It's not a winning strategy. Be the better person. That's the way to win. Prove to yourself – not to them, but to yourself – just how amazingly amazing you can be. That's the best strategy.

"Love thy neighbor as thyself." What an ideal to strive for!

And remember, the statements, "I love my neighbor" and "My neighbor is kind of an asshole sometimes" are not mutually exclusive. You can still love someone even though they are kind of an asshole. People do it all the time! (Um, but let's try to keep our relationships healthy here...)

You can love your neighbor's *humanity*, even if you also disapprove of some of the things your neighbor says or does. My neighbor, for his part, regularly brings us fruits and vegetables from his garden at harvest time: huge bags full of tomatoes or zucchini or whatever happens to be in season. How can I hold a grudge against a guy like that? I can't. If I do, it's my own fault. The lesson here is, you can love your neighbor by focusing on what is good about them; and you can get your neighbors to love you by giving them the fruits of your garden (literally or figuratively), or whatever you have to offer.

"Love your enemies, do good to them which hate you, bless them that curse you, and pray for them which despitefully use you. And unto him that smiteth thee on the one cheek, offer also the other; and to one who taketh away thy shirt, offer thy coat also. Give to everyone that asketh of thee." (as Luke 6:27-30)

And as Thich Nhat Hanh reminds us, if we were in their place, we would probably do the same as them.

That's what it means to love people. It means to love everyone: even those who hurt you, even if they continue to hurt you.

And that can be hard to do. Oh, yes, it's really hard! That's why this is a practice. Personal transformation is not just something you do once. It is a process. It is a choice. We return to it, over and over.

Now, turning the other cheek is a rousing metaphor; but in real life, you should probably try to defend yourself, or get away. You should not just stand there and allow someone to abuse you like that, if you have the choice. You can say, "forgive them, for they know not what they do," but that doesn't mean you have to let them keep doing it. Take action. Make them stop if you can, or leave the situation if you must.

Nonetheless, the larger point is clear. When we entertain thoughts of revenge, we harm ourselves. By focusing on our grievances, we allow our minds to spiral down to dark places.

In another example from a major world religion, *The Dhammapada* is among the most ancient surviving Buddhist texts, and believed to be closely based on the actual words of the Buddha.

The very first psalm in this foundational collection warns about the trap of the victim mentality:

'He insulted me, he struck me,
    he defeated me, he robbed me':
  for those who get caught up in this,
    hatred does not cease.
'He insulted me, he struck me,
    he defeated me, he robbed me':
  for those who do *not* get caught up in this,
    hatred ceases completely.[8]

I believe it is not a coincidence that early Buddhist teachings are so similar to the teachings of Jesus in this respect. On that level, both philosophies are part of a larger current of thought within humanity's long-term and ever-developing social awareness. Parallel concepts are to be found in the teachings of Hinduism, Zoroastrianism, and more.

These ideas are universal because this is something we all need to learn: everyone, everywhere, around the world and throughout time. It's not just you. It's not just me. It's all of us. So let's do this together. Let's make a change.

Let's start today.

---

8   *The Dhammapada*, I.1:2-3. Translation by Valerie J. Roebuck. Emphasis added.

3.2 Forgive People

Oh, this is a tough one.

Forgiveness is a forgotten value in our modern culture.

Forgive yourself, and forgive others.

Stand up for yourself, if you must! But don't get sucked into an endless cycle of reactions, retaliations, and recriminations. It's better to focus on your core values, your personal sense of purpose, and the pursuit of your larger life goals.

Whatever shit went down, there's no sense in dwelling on it. It's done.

Shame is a form of blame; and blame is a form of hate. These are "catch and release" emotions. That is to say, they come to most of us, at times; but when they arrive, we must not hold onto them. As soon as we experience them, we must recognize them for what they are, and let them go.

Whether you blame yourself, or you blame someone else: either way you're focusing on, and projecting, negative emotions. When we dwell in that place, we can't heal. If we can't heal, then we're going to continue experiencing thought spirals, painful emotions, and occasional explosions when we lash out and vent our resentment in unhealthy ways: whether through sarcastic remarks, or passive-aggressive undermining, or overtly aggressive behavior, or perhaps self-destructive behavior. Does this sound familiar? If you have exhibited negative behaviors in the past, then you know you don't want to return to that mental space in the future. You remember how you felt when you were constantly criticizing others because deep down you hated yourself. You can remove yourself from the mental place you were in when you were exhibiting that behavior. You can break that cycle now: by loving yourself, by forgiving yourself, and by loving and forgiving everyone else.

Forgive those who have wronged you. Sure, someone has wronged you in the past: we have all been wronged at some point in our lives. But dwelling in that space, lingering in the mentality of a victim: it leaves you powerless, or even worse, it makes you obsessed with thoughts of revenge.

Revenge is not justice. In fact, because "justice" is so abstract, and such a moving target, you may never feel that it has been completely achieved. You're going to have to learn to accept that. You are not a court of law; and if you try too hard to achieve some abstract notion of justice, there is a one hundred percent chance that you will make things worse. So don't attach your hopes to abstractions and impossibilities.

Justice (according to Christopher Nolan's *Batman Begins*, which ranks as one of my favorite movies of all time) is a quest for balance; whereas revenge is an expression of the ego. Preventing future harm is a function of justice; but intentionally causing harm to someone you hate is pure vindictiveness.

Vindictiveness, vengefulness, and schadenfreude[9] are all expressions of hate: and in the long term, they will only cause more pain and suffering. As mindful human beings, we must not intentionally cause suffering. Instead, let us pursue healing, and make the world a better place.

Everyone has been hurt at some time; and everyone has hurt someone else at some time. Pursuing revenge is the worst possible solution for this problem: because it perpetuates the cycle.

---

9   "Schadenfreude" (a.k.a. "lolz") is the fancy term for taking pleasure in witnessing the pain and suffering of another person: like that YouTube video you watched with the word "karma" in the title, for example.

The Buddhist monk and internationally renowned peace activist Thich Nhat Hanh was one of the greatest teachers of our modern times. In his book *Peace is Every Step*, Hanh discusses an exercise he practiced to feel empathy for a man who had committed a terrible crime. The empathy does not excuse the crime. The empathy does not make the crime any less terrible. The empathy only recognizes the fundamental humanity which the pacifist monk shares with the violent criminal.

It's important to remember the basic humanity of other people. No matter how badly they may have hurt us, they share our basic humanity.

As Brené Brown writes in *Rising Strong*, most people are usually doing their best.[10] That's a powerful thought. Or as I like to say, all people are simply people, everywhere and throughout time. We are all the same.

So focus your mind on forgiveness. Let go of the negative emotion that keeps you feeling wronged: because as long as your mind is consumed by thoughts of how you have been wronged, then you are more likely to lash out and cause harm. That's not how you want to

---

10   This key concept of Brown's work has also been widely
     discussed by other thought leaders.

live. Heal yourself, and heal your relationship with the world, and set your feet on the path of love.

Redemption is possible.

Forgiveness is divine.

3.2.1 Case Study: Blamed for the Breakup

After The Beatles split up, all the other group members blamed it on Paul McCartney. It turned into a huge long-running grievance. The other three rock stars spent years carrying around a sense of rage against Paul. The drama attracted something of a media circus at the time.

John Lennon even wrote several songs talking shit about Paul; and to really make it sting, the other two former Beatles bandmates (George and Ringo) joined John to record those songs for his new album. John's songs lobbed accusations such as, "All you ever did was Yesterday," saying (on the face of it) that Paul's best work was all in the past; but also making an obvious pun on the title of one of Paul's best songs: and thereby implying that the song in question was Paul's sole claim to fame: an obvious falsehood, because (like John Lennon)

Paul McCartney was one of the greatest, most prolific songwriters of the Twentieth Century.

McCartney, to his credit, seems to have been much more subtle in his messaging, and refrained from the sort of direct attacks that John engaged in. My point here is that Paul McCartney must have felt very personally hurt and rejected by all this. The three guys who he had built a life with; his three best friends, creative collaborators, and business partners: they all hated him, apparently, and now they were singing songs about how much they hated him. They were saying these things in public, on popular record albums, in songs that got played on the radio to an international audience of millions.

Now, Paul McCartney was a sweet, sensitive, caring guy: the kind of guy who would write a song like, "When I'm Sixty-Four." He was not the kind of guy who normally found himself at the center of massively controversial, high-profile personal disputes. Drama and grandstanding were more sort of John Lennon's game.

To make matters worse, if you look at the situation objectively, it seems clear that John Lennon had played a key role in sabotaging the relationship. Watch the movie of *The Magical*

Mystery Tour, and observe John through the second half of the film. Apparently, during the filming, John and George Harrison disappeared for several hours during the afternoon, presumably to go get high; and when they came back, they sat apart from all the others, slouched back, arms folded across chests, John occasionally leaning over to murmur a cynical remark to George; all while Paul and Ringo did all the work, entertaining the guests and making the movie they were getting paid to make. Of course, I love John Lennon, and in any given moment of real life, there's always more going on than a single camera angle can capture. But it seems very clear that it was really unfair of John to blame the band's breakup entirely on Paul, when it appears that John had been making things difficult for years.

If you have been slandered by your former friends; if you have been publicly mocked, shamed, dragged through the mud, and vilified in mass media broadcasts: you are not alone. It also happened to Paul McCartney, all-round decent fellow and one of the greatest songwriters of the Twentieth Century.

After this difficult time, Paul went on to start a new band, write more great songs, and pursue a fulfilling career as a musician and entertainer.

Eventually, Paul was reconciled with the other former Beatles.

The story my parents told me when I was a kid is, after years of all of this bullshit and backstabbing, **one day John showed up at Paul's house with a guitar in his hand**. I don't know if John apologized, in so many words. I don't know if saying the actual words really even matters all that much. Either way, Paul accepted John's apology, because Paul was a gentle, forgiving soul.

Paul forgave John.

After everything John had said about him, Paul still forgave him.

Decades later, long after John was murdered, Paul got together with the other surviving members of the group, to play their old songs live in concert.

Paul forgave George and Ringo, too.

None of that really makes up for the pain that Paul went through when his former friends slandered him so publicly. But eventually the world for the most part seems to have forgotten about the controversy, and many people now recognize that all of John's high-profile shit-talking about Paul was nothing more than the unjustified slanderous rantings of a heroin addict.

So if you're in a rough spot now, that's important to remember. In a few years no one will care; and eventually you may even be more or less vindicated in public opinion.

3.3 Believe in People

There is value in rediscovering our faith in humanity.

All people are just people, around the world and throughout time. If we are to basically believe in ourselves and our own fundamental decency, then we must also begin to believe in the fundamental decency of others in general. Yes, some are better than others, so we must protect ourselves; but we must also focus on the positive. We must allow ourselves to have faith. We must give ourselves permission to hope.

It can be difficult to believe in people after you have been hurt; but finding it in your heart to believe in others may be the key to believing in yourself again. After all, other people are people just like you. Sometimes we are stupid or selfish. But in our moments of incandescence we attain redemption. We rise above. We carry on. We move forward. We do our best. We keep trying, even when it's hard. We keep striving, even when success is uncertain. We keep going. This is who we are, this is what we do.

As Lao Tzu wrote in the *Tao Te Ching*:

"I am good to people who are good.
 I am also good to people who are not good,
 Because Virtue is goodness.
 I have faith in people who are faithful.
 I also have faith in people who are not faithful,
 Because Virtue is faithfulness."[11]

Assume positive intent on the part of others. That can be difficult when you've had negative experiences, because of the mind's negativity bias: but most people are basically decent. Rather than always assuming that others are trying to hurt you, assume they mean well, or at least that they're essentially harmless. Relate to them on a level of mutual self-interest; and if you can't help them, say so. Say what you want. Be direct.

Learn to work well with others.

---

11 Chapter 49

3.3.1 Case Study: Greatness Through Collaboration

As the turn of the millennium approached, Carlos Santana felt himself growing increasingly irrelevant.

It had been three decades since his iconic, career-defining performance at the Woodstock festival; and much time had passed. He was getting older. He was playing a genre of music that has rarely (if ever) been chart-topping. In fact, his music was kind of difficult to define: it was a fusion of Latin and rock styles, and he played a lot of instrumental songs. It's not the sort of stuff that typically goes to the top of the charts, so it's remarkable that he'd already had several hits in the past. But by now, his handful of well-known songs were all 25 or 30 years old, and his future career seemed uncertain.

So Carlos Santana redefined himself.

And he did it by believing in other people.

Santana collaborated with a whole album's worth of (mostly) younger performers, people who were at the top of their game: from Y Clef Jean to Dave Matthews and even Eric Clapton, and put together the chart-topping album, *Supernatural*.

That album produced some of the greatest hits of Santana's career. *Supernatural* introduced Santana to a whole new generation of fans. The project made Carlos Santana more internationally popular than he had ever been before.

And he did this by rethinking the possibilities of the situation. He did this by connecting with others through music. Santana considered new ways of being, new ways of expressing himself, and collaborative partnerships with other people – even people who were known for playing musical styles far outside of his usual genre. The collaborative musical partnerships that he put together with these other creatives produced some of the greatest work of his career, the work he became best known for in the next decades.

So if you're feeling like your best work is behind you, and you feel like what you're known for is something you did a long time ago, and you're beginning to see little hope in your future: just remember Carlos Santana. Be like Carlos Santana. Redefine yourself. Introduce yourself to a new generation of people, using new techniques and exploring new styles, but putting your own personal touch on those styles. Remember, although he redefined himself,

Santana did not try to become someone else. No, this was a study in that overused buzzword, "authenticity." Santana continued to play the same kind of music that Santana had always played; but he achieved a creative fusion of his style with the styles of all these other musicians, and in the process he was able to come up with something completely new, something beautiful, something incredible, something that really touched people, and it improved a lot of people's lives, being able to listen to this amazing music; and it certainly turned Santana's career around and gave him a whole new life.

Santana revived his career and created himself anew at an age when most aging rockers just fade, and he did it by connecting with other musicians. You can't do this alone. Connecting with other people is the key to your new life.

So be like Carlos Santana. Believe in people. Work with people. Take a look around and see what currently isn't being done, and do it, and become indispensable to people. People will love you for it.

3.4 Living With Integrity

Integrity is doing what we say we will do; behaving in the way we expect others to behave;

openness, honesty, and straight talk; fulfilling our obligations; learning from our mistakes; and living in accordance with our own principles and core values.

In order to live with integrity and get along well with others, we should assume responsibility for what we can control.

A core premise of self-help is, "You can only control yourself." And yet this notion offers hope! You can consciously change your own future, if you take responsibility for changing your future. It is empowering to believe that our choices in the present can affect our experience in the future. Above all, we must take responsibility for our own words and actions.

That's why traditional faiths have so many religious injunctions centered around contract law, the upholding of oaths, and prohibitions against false swearing and false accusations. To live with integrity, we should do what we say we're going to do; and we should fulfill our obligations to others.

One way of safeguarding ourselves, is to avoid encumbering ourselves with obligations.

If someone else accuses you of letting them down or breaking your word in some way, avoid arguing with them about it. This can be difficult or even painful sometimes. That's why this message has been taught by world religions for thousands of years. For example, the *Tao Te Ching* counsels:

"Easy promises make for little trust.
 Taking things lightly results in great difficulty."[12]

In just this same vein, we are told that Jesus said,

"It was said in days of old, 'You shall not swear falsely, but shall perform what you have sworn.' But I say unto you: Do not swear at all! Neither by heaven, nor by the earth, nor by your own head. Let what you say be simply 'Yes' or 'No.'" (abridged, based on Matthew 5:33-37)

I think this is important for us all to remember.

Avoid making statements; avoid making promises. Above all, avoid explaining yourself.

If you find that you're explaining yourself a lot, then you probably have a bad habit of opening your mouth when you should keep quiet: just as I do. You and I both need to learn to avoid the trap of filling awkward silences with even more awkward gaffes. (In *Never Split the*

---

12 Chapter 63

Difference, hostage negotiator Chris Voss reveals that simply refraining from saying anything for a few extra moments can be a winning negotiation technique, even in mundane situations such as buying a car.) Let go of the need to be the next one to speak. Instead, focus on your breath, and enjoy the present moment. If someone else is going on and on and on, just let them. (Unless their train of thought becomes too negative, in which case I think it's reasonable to redirect the conversation to more constructive territory.)

Avoid making statements of fact, unless it's your job to make statements. Facts generally stand on their own, yet they are frequently misinterpreted. The world does not require a constant stream of all your judgments.

Whether you're required to make a statement of fact in a business context, or it's your turn to relate a personal anecdote in a social setting: whatever the situation, be careful to avoid either exaggeration or minimization. (That said, human memory is notoriously fallible, and our perception is demonstrably prone to misinterpretation; so if you catch someone else in an exaggeration, just let it go, this is not generally a reflection on their character.)

Avoid providing numeric estimates of anything. (If you're writing a research paper, you can cite your sources; but in casual conversation, words like "a few" or "many" are generally sufficient to get your point across; and in business, I find that most customers greatly prefer fixed prices over the estimate-based model.)

Do what you say you're going to do. This is the core of integrity.

Nobody wants to be known as the sort of person who makes commitments that they can't keep; but if you make too many promises, you will eventually find yourself unable to fulfill them all. Therefore, in order to avoid over-promising, you should break the nasty habit of telling people what you think they want to hear. That's a tough one, I know, but it's necessary.

Furthermore, break the habit of telling people your plans for everything you're going to do in the future – unless you're specifically trying to *get them to help you* do it. Rather than telling people what you're going to do, just go do it. If it's your own goal, you can tell people about it after you've achieved it; and if it's something you're doing for others, they'll notice after you've done it. That way, if it takes longer than you expected or your plans change for any reason, you won't be stuck apologizing or explaining, because you hadn't promised anything to anyone.

Let it be your intent to constantly surprise people with the excellence of all you have done; but try not to be personally offended if they fail to notice how amazing you are: after all, they are all living in their own minds, just like you. (And that's why on rare occasions it's necessary to be a bit "self-promotional" and "toot your own horn" for your accomplishments, humility be damned – but we must be careful not to do this to excess, for it quickly wears others out.)

Small details can make a big difference. The next time complexity arises in your life or decisions, may you see a clear path to living in alignment with your core values. May you apply the same principles to your present situation that you would apply to the same situation if it were reversed. That's a level of integrity that we can all aspire to; and if we ever fall short, we can aspire to do better next time.

We should strive to apply the same rules to ourselves that we apply to others. We should strive to apply the same rules in different situations and with different people. We should strive to follow the same rules that we expect others to obey. We should strive to hold ourselves to high standards of truthfulness and ethical behavior.

As the *Tao Te Ching* recommends,

"Knowing constancy, the mind is open.
  With an open mind, you will be openhearted.
  Being openhearted, you will act generously.
  Being generous, you will attain the divine."[13]

3.4.1 Do What Is Asked of You (Within Reason)

"You're right." "I'm sorry." "That was my mistake." "No worries." "Go ahead." "I'd be happy to." "As you wish." "You're welcome." "Thank you."

Sometimes it almost **hurts** to say some of these, especially when we're certain the other person is in the wrong; and that's understandable. Nonetheless, the more comfortable we get with saying them effortlessly, even when we think the other person might not entirely deserve it: the more effortlessly we tend to go through life.

In his famous Sermon on the Mount speech, Jesus said,

---

13 Chapter 16. My translation has "royally," but I believe "generously" may be closer to a modern understanding of the verse's meaning.

"Agree with thine adversary quickly... lest at any time the adversary deliver thee to the judge, and the judge deliver thee to the officer, and thou be cast in prison." (Matthew 5:25)

Thankfully, we no longer have debtor's prisons; but the core principle remains the same. There are *consequences* if we fail to meet our promises and obligations. When someone makes a claim against us, the simplest and quickest resolution is usually to agree with them. Don't argue with them. **Even if you're sure they are wrong**, arguing about it is generally pointless and counterproductive. Just do the shit and get it over with.

The *Tao Te Ching* offers remarkably similar advice:

"After a bitter quarrel, resentment lingers.
 How can this be considered a win?
 Therefore,
 The wise keep their half of the bargain,
 but do not exact their due.
 Virtuous people fulfill their obligations;
   but those without Virtue make demands of others."[14]

----

14 Chapter 79. Paraphrase informed by multiple translations.

Lao Tzu is even more blunt in a later passage:

"Good people do not argue.
  Those who argue are not good."[15]

Well, I have spent a lot of my life arguing; so I guess I still have a long way to go. It's a process.

Heck, I spend a lot of this book arguing in favor of the principles of self-help. I believe there's a place for making a point!

But in the field of interpersonal relations, let's do our best to set controversy aside.

Is this a court of law? If not, what does it matter what you can "prove"?

Generally, it's more important to maintain strong, supportive, loving relationships.

Be the person who does more than is asked.

As we are told that Jesus taught:

"If any one would sue you in a court of law and take your shirt, give him your coat, as well. And if any one forces you to go one mile, go with him two miles. Give to all who ask of you, and lend to those who need your help." (slight paraphrase based on Matthew 5:40-42)

---

15   *Tao Te Ching*, Chapter 81.

In this passage Jesus is saying, basically, "If someone demands money from you, pay it to them."

Note that Jesus does *not* say, "You owe this person money because it's all your fault." There's no notion of guilt or blame attached to his admonition. Whether or not you believe you legitimately owe this other person money is irrelevant. On the contrary: this passage is part of a long series of injunctions instructing us to accept the injustices imposed upon us by others. In fact, this passage immediately follows the most famous injunction from the same Sermon, in which Jesus instructs us to "turn the other cheek."

"You have heard it said, 'An eye for an eye and a tooth for a tooth.' But I say to you, Do not resist evil, but if any one strikes you on the right cheek, turn to him the other also." (slight paraphrase of Matthew 5:38-39)

Again, Jesus is not claiming that you *deserve* to be struck. **This is not what you deserve.** On the contrary: You deserve to be treated humanely at all times. I think we can all agree that if someone strikes you, they have seriously crossed the line! Again, no notion of guilt or blame attaches to this admonition. This is not about "karma," or "justice," or what you "deserve," or what someone else "deserves." Jesus was advocating a philosophy of extreme passivity: the pursuit of conflict avoidance as a path to peace.

The lesson is clear: We must do what is required of us, and sometimes it will feel unjust. There's no sense in complaining about it or scheming for revenge. Don't adopt a martyr complex. Holding onto grudges poisons the mind. Lest we spiral down a deep dark hole of blame and hatred, we must learn to **forgive** those who have hurt us.

3.4.2 Enforce Firm Boundaries

As with most advice, we must temper the above with practicality. If followed to the letter on a daily basis, this advice is a great way to get hurt, crushed, taken advantage of by the unscrupulous, and oppressed by the power-hungry.

I generally reject labels like "empath," "people pleaser" and "giver," just as I reject labels like "toxic" and "taker." It's overly simplistic, and far too often these labels are misapplied in a headfuck effort to make an aggressor seem like a victim and vice-versa. Remember, we're not here to judge; and if we're not judging, then we must not call people names: not even ourselves. Instead, we examine behaviors, relationships, and outcomes. If a given behavior contributes to an unhealthy relationship or an undesirable outcome, then we can choose to change that behavior. This is the path to a better future.

Many people who find themselves at rock bottom begin to feel so abject that they accept blame for things that are **not their fault**. We begin to reflexively apologize as a defense mechanism. Unfortunately, this does not engender respect in our peers and companions: on the contrary, it encourages them to walk all over us.

Having empathy for others does not remove the need to enforce firm boundaries. This sometimes seems like a contradiction, so it's important to consider the distinction.

You get more of what you tolerate; and we must never tolerate the intolerable.

What people consider "intolerable" has changed throughout time, but it most commonly involves some form of violence or coercion.

As free and independent human beings, we must never silently suffer mistreatment at the hands of anyone. We must never allow ourselves to remain in a situation where we are being actively harmed by another person. You can forgive them and still ask that they cease their misbehavior and even be held accountable for their actions. You can understand how badly they have been hurt in their own life without tolerating their bad behavior against you. You can have empathy for the factors that brought them to whatever dark place they are in in their life; but that does not mean that you have to let them take it out on you. You must protect yourself. Protect yourself from physical harm, and protect yourself from psychological harm.

If you are in an abusive relationship, the time to get out is now.

At some point, loving one another requires us to set and maintain boundaries.

Being good to others doesn't mean always giving others what they ask for.

For example, we might have to deny a request if they ask for something that is not good for them: such as when my teenager wants to eat ice cream instead of dinner. Thus, even in the context of being good to others, we still must set, communicate, and enforce reasonable boundaries.

We also must ensure that our own needs are being met. Remember, I'm not treating myself well if I drain myself or my resources by always giving you everything you ask for. That's disrespectful to me. Thus, sometimes prudence demands that we must tell others, "No."

We have to find a balance. Sometimes self-care requires us to set boundaries and maintain them against the demands of others. Just do what needs to be done.

You can understand that the quest for balance is ongoing; and you can start today.

3.4.3 Seek Balance

As human beings navigating a complex society, we are daily challenged to exercise situational discretion, and to seek balance.

In the present context, we must balance the imperative to kindness against the imperative to enforce boundaries. In some situations we will tend to lean one way, in some situations we may lean the other way. Not every situation is the same.

Recall the Flipper Factor: you don't need flippers if you're skydiving. Advice is situational.

More broadly, we seek balance in all things, even as we realize that balance itself cannot remain static for long because all things are always in a state of flux.

As Lao Tzu describes it in the *Tao Te Ching*, all of creation exists in a state of tension between two opposing forces: *yin* and *yang*; or push and pull, if you will; or male and female, to use a familiar analogy; but just as accurately, "this" and "that." To categorize these forces in human terms would be to anthropomorphize something that's fundamentally beyond human understanding. They are simply the one, and the other. Neither force is good or evil. Both forces are essential to the existence of the universe.

Modern physics posits a similar tension between the attractive force of gravity, which arguably creates matter as we understand it, and the repulsion force of Dark Energy, which apparently creates the space between the matter, and allows things to be distinct from one another (just as primal deities separate the Earth from the Sky in creation myths from Sumeria and ancient Egypt to Mesoamerica). The existence of reality as we know it depends on both of these forces in a perpetual state of tension. But whether you prefer ancient

Chinese mysticism or complex astro-mathematical equations, you will eventually come to the realization that the "balance" of these cosmic forces is never static: it is continually in a state of flux.

"For one gains by losing, and loses by gaining." (*Tao Te Ching*, Chapter 42)

You might envision the complex area of interaction between these forces as the intricate interplay of a dance, eternally in motion. One or the other of the forces is continually invading the space of the other, or retreating in the face of the other's advance: and then trading places, sort of, although the patterns are ever-changing as the forces swirl about. This is the structure of our universe; and it is in this ever-changing environment that we must seek, and create, what balance we can.

Here are some more examples of seeking balance and enforcing boundaries.

If someone asks you for something, give it to them, if you can; but exercise good stewardship of your time and resources, so you can live in reasonable comfort and security and meet your obligations.

Listen to criticism, but don't take things personally: especially when some toxic critic insults you personally and tries to make you feel bad about yourself, because this form of criticism says more about the critic than it says about you.

Pay people what you owe them, deal fairly in business, and tip generously; but don't be gullible or allow others to take advantage of you, for that causes long-term harm to yourself and to your family.

Accept responsibility for your mistakes, for your life situation, and above all for what your future holds in store; but don't dwell on your failures or go around agonizing about everything you've done wrong, because nobody wants to hear that shit, with the notable exception of assholes who will be sure to use it against you in the future.

Be tolerant of others; but remember that you get more of what you tolerate: so enforce firm boundaries, and say "no" like you mean it.

Furthermore, in common practice, you may find that the advice you hear in life is often more directly pertinent to the offerer than to the recipient. It's important for us to learn to trust our own judgment for this reason.

Learn to trust your own judgment. You are a decent person. Keep doing that.

Part 4: Thinking About Thoughts

Thoughts are a natural byproduct of human biology.

So are turds.

Thoughts, like turds, are merely an inevitable byproduct of being alive and human.

Of course, not all thoughts *are* turds. Some thoughts are extremely valuable! But many of our thoughts simply need to be flushed and forgotten: especially when we are experiencing a dark time in our lives.

As you get deeper into self-help, you begin to notice a strong connection between self-help and such practices and concepts as mindfulness, meditation, and the latest fancy buzzword, "Emotional Intelligence." Meditation has been integral to Eastern spiritual and religious practices for thousands of years, for a good reason. These concepts have such a practical application that we now hear them commonly recommended by business coaches.

One of the key principles of meditation is this: You are not your thoughts.

This is important because so often we tend to identify with our thoughts. That's an especially serious problem for trauma survivors, or for anyone who has even *approached* rock bottom. When we identify with thoughts that are dark, disturbing, or fearful, then we become deeply convinced that there is something seriously wrong with us (or with the world, or both): and that conviction can quickly send us down a dark spiral.

But the truth is, everybody has disturbing thoughts sometimes. It's not just you.

You are not your thoughts. The fact that you have disturbing thoughts sometimes is not a reflection on your character, or your fate. "Demons" are merely a metaphor, and you have the power to overcome your own inner demons. You just need to learn some new ways of thinking.

The very real problem, as anyone who has experienced depression or anxiety knows, is that when we are afflicted by disturbing thoughts, those thoughts reverberate and circle back and recur until they become so loud that we have trouble focusing on the present or enjoying anything in life. People who have not been at rock bottom may not understand what this is like. I once wrote a poem[16] that compared my intrusive thoughts to

> "...a hammer
> that's loudly pounding on a sheet of brass,
> insistent, constant, ringing and noisy,
> pounding, pounding within your very skull,
> defiling all that's beautiful in life."

If that experience sounds at all familiar to you, then you and I have something in common.

The same poem complains that our uncaring peers like to offer us unhelpful advice along the lines of "Just don't think about it." That kind of so-called "advice" is unhelpful because, as George Lakoff indicated in the famous title, *Don't Think of an Elephant!*, it's essentially impossible to *not* think about something. The harder we try to "not think about it," the more strongly the mind conjures more thoughts of the subject in question! By trying to "not think about" something, we indicate to the mind that the subject is important, and the disturbing thought perversely resurfaces ever more persistently.

---

16 "Intrusive Thoughts" from the collection *A Year Outside of Time*, published under my pen name, Titus Naso.

The only workable solution is to think about something else, instead.

Think about gratitude. Think about the sunrise. Think about people who have been kind to you. Think about all the ways you want to show kindness to others. Think about your goals. Think about your purpose. Think about what you love. Think about goodness.

Alternatively, focus on your breath. Focus on a mandala. Focus on the sensation of touching your fingertips together. Focus on whatever pleases you. Focus your awareness on this present moment so intently that there's no space left in your mind for any other thoughts.

Of course, even the most experienced meditators can only do this for a while before thoughts surface. This does not mean that you're "doing it wrong." It merely indicates that your brain is still functional. Thoughts will arise: it is inevitable. Don't beat yourself up over it. When those thoughts do surface, as Dan Harris discusses in *Meditation for Fidgety Skeptics*, simply recognize them, acknowledge to yourself that you are thinking, congratulate yourself for being aware that you are thinking, and set the thoughts aside so you can return to your focus on the present moment.

Given my childhood experiences, I have long had an interest in the workings of the human mind.

I took an Intro to Psychology course in college, but I was disappointed to discover that the class was all Freud and abnormal diagnoses. The course didn't teach me what I wanted to know. I wanted to understand human nature, motivations, and decision-making: which is, after all, probably too big a question to be easily or succinctly answered, just like the original vaguely worded question posed to the supercomputer Deep Thought in Douglas Adams' *The Hitchhiker's Guide to the Galaxy*.

I got a much more specific answer from the classes I took for my MBA in Marketing, more than a decade later. My favorite textbook was *Consumer Behavior: Buying, Having, and Being (Ninth Edition)* by Michael R. Solomon. From Solomon, I learned that we humans are motivated by emotion, and by memory associations, far more than by any sort of rational decision-making process. We believe we are rational creatures; but in practice, we are primarily motivated by our feelings, and we invent rationalizations (after the fact) to explain why we felt like doing whatever it was.

But once you begin to think about human motivations in these terms, you can easily see that it's not only our advertising and marketing industry that's designed to try to get inside your memory, evoke an emotional response, and thus affect your decision-making process: it's also the news media, and the social media, and the fringe political views that seem to be increasingly socially acceptable these days, but my publisher says I'm not supposed to talk about that in this book, oh wait my publisher is me.

That last paragraph was a demonstration.

The mind just goes, and goes, and goes, and goes, doesn't it? Free association! Sometimes the thought stream offers comments on its own commentary at a speed many times faster than mere speech could ever hope to rival.

There is surely an evolutionary advantage to this trait of the endless mental commentary; and yet (as Ethan Kross discusses in his book *Chatter*) mental chatter can prove distracting or even unnecessarily distressing in a modern context.

In order to gain control of our thoughts, it often helps to understand our own thoughts. That way, when we begin to have these thoughts – or we begin to have the types of thoughts that often lead to these thoughts – we can choose to redirect a conversation or our mental energy to... greener pastures.

This is, after all, the purpose of the exercise of meditation, as developed by practitioners of Eastern philosophies and religions such as Hinduism, Buddhism, and Taoism.

Eventually, I got into self-help, and enjoyed the benefits of many books, audiobooks, podcasts, YouTube videos, and apps. From the writings and talks of Buddhist monks, and Stoic philosophers, and clinical psychologists, and even a six-week "Positive Intelligence" online seminar with Shirzad Chamine (courtesy of coaching guru Chris Lalchan), I learned a variety of techniques and perspectives related to intentionally asserting control over our otherwise habitual and automatic emotional responses, so that we may be more slow to anger, and quick to give gifts, for example. This is a key insight of personal transformation.

The specifics of the techniques for refocusing the mind are discussed in detail by, among others, Dan Harris and Jeff Warren in *Meditation for Fidgety Skeptics*. The basic principle is to focus on something (your breath, a mantra, some meditation music) so intently that your awareness is entirely filled with an appreciation of whatever it is you are focusing on, and your mind ceases to pursue any train of thought: not an analysis of whatever you are focusing on, not a rehearsal of the past or plans for the future, not a commentary on anything, not a complaint about anything, just a pure focus on your breath or whatever you have chosen to focus on. I can usually do it for a few seconds at best. The first time I was able to do it at all, no matter how briefly, felt like a huge breakthrough. At last I was beginning to gain control over the thoughts that had tormented me for years.

Another aspect of gaining control of our thoughts, is to understand our own thoughts better.

Towards that end, here are a few specific types of thoughts to be aware of. When you notice yourself having one of these thoughts, it doesn't mean anything: it's just an opportunity for you to ask yourself why you're having this thought, whether you really agree with this thought, whether this is a thought worth focusing your energy on; and if not, it's an opportunity for you to consciously, intentionally choose to focus your thoughts on something else. And if negative thoughts are persistent, that's an opportunity for you to pursue a meditation exercise or perhaps a therapeutic approach, whatever works for you.

So, with that stated intent, let's talk about a few types of thoughts you may be familiar with.

4.1 Thinking in Extremes

In *Change Your Brain, Change Your Life*, Daniel Amen offers a list of some types of thoughts which we often allow to become our pessimistic defaults. Dr. Amen describes these as "Automatic Negative Thoughts," and advises us to be on the lookout for these types of thoughts when they arise, so that we may actively choose to focus our attention on positive thoughts, instead.

One of the examples Dr. Amen emphasizes is extreme thinking: that is, thoughts that judge situations or people as being either entirely one thing or completely the opposite, with no nuance or middle ground. For example, in a down moment, we might say of ourselves, "I'm the worst ever." Or, we might casually state in conversation that something "always" happens, or that something else "never" happens. Words like "always," "never," and "worst" are warning signs of extreme thoughts.

We should be on the lookout for our tendency to think in extremes: because such thoughts tend to lead us astray. When such thoughts arise, remember to seek balance, and nuance, and the gray area.

4.2 Perseveration and Rumination

Ever had a thought that just wouldn't leave you alone? Or worse, a thought spiral that seemed to pull you endlessly down to a bottomless pit? Yeah, you know what I'm talking about. I'm pretty sure we have all experienced this in some form, although of course... some of us more than others.

We perseverate on our fears and anxiety for the future; and we ruminate on our regrets, grievances, shame, and anger about the past. We mull these thoughts over, and over, and over, and get stressed, and lie awake at night, and replay conversations, or imagine conversations or scenarios.

When worries, fears, regrets, grievances, past pain, and other negative thoughts recur over and over to the point where they completely torment us and seriously interfere with our enjoyment of the present: this is a sign that it's time for us to gain control over our own thoughts.

Breaking decades-long thought patterns is possible! There are brighter days on the other side of this process.

4.2.1 Focus on the Moment

Part of what's so wonderful about being human is our ability to reminisce about the past and dream about the future.

But part of what's worst about being stuck in a bad place in our lives is that we become consumed by memories of our past pain, and by our fear and anxiety about the future.

So if you're stuck right now, then part of what you need to do to turn your life around, is to let go of your worries and fears, your regrets and your grievances. Oh, yes, believe me, I know: that's easier said than done. And that's why it's so important.

One tool for chipping away at the thick layer of mental bullshit that currently coats your life, is meditation.

Just focus your awareness so intently on one thing – usually your breathing – that your thoughts recede into the background.

If you are focusing on your breath, remember that you're just observing it. Breathe naturally. As the *Tao Te Ching* observes, "Trying to control the breath causes strain."[17]

Now, thoughts will attempt to arise, one after another after another. You cannot stop your mind from popping up with new thoughts all the time, like popcorn, pop pop pop; so just recognize the thoughts, perhaps try to identify their source and thereby understand yourself (and your triggers) a little better; and finally, set the thoughts aside without judgment, and return your awareness to a focus on your breathing.

Full disclosure: I have found meditation difficult. If you have tried meditation in the past and found it difficult, it's not just you. My mind wanders. I had to come back to it for many repeated attempts, some of them in guided sessions through an app on my phone, before I was able to turn off my mental chatter for even just a few seconds. I still don't meditate daily, and when I do, it's rarely for longer than ten minutes, and I usually listen to guided meditations. So I'm hardly an ideal spokesperson for this movement. And yet, I believe even the minimal amount of meditation practice that I've done, has already made a noticeable difference for me.

---

17 Chapter 55

Which is why I strongly recommend that you try meditation: and don't give up if you can't do it the first time, because you won't be able to do it the first time. You probably still won't be able to do it the thirtieth time, either, but you will begin to get better. You don't have to spend hours at it every day, you are not a monk (unless you are a monk, in which case, enjoy!). But I believe you will find that even just a small amount of meditation practice – brief, occasional sessions – can yield huge rewards over time.

We all need to develop this skill, the ability to stay centered and calm in the midst of a storm of chaos. We need this skill because it's difficult to feel centered when you've got kids screaming at you and a bunch of stuff going on: the phone ringing, and the dog barking, and the alarm going off, and things you have to do, and things that you haven't done yet, and things you have to get ready for. It's difficult to feel centered in that time: that takes a lot of practice.

It's a lot easier to feel centered when you can get outside and you can see the stars. You can see the silhouettes of the trees against the darkening sky, and you breathe the crisp cool evening air, and you feel yourself to be connected with the great Universe around you,

You are one with the whole entire Cosmos, you are just a very small part of it: you are a very small part of a very big picture, and you can feel that. It's easier to feel that when you're at peace, when you're able to feel peace and experience peace because of the peaceful world outside you. So do yourself a favor. Break your routine sometimes. Get outside and enjoy the fresh air. Go spend some time in Nature. Remember how it feels to breathe in peace.

But the real trick is always going to be to learn how to find peace within, no matter where you are or what you're doing. Since we have commitments and obligations, we can't always drop whatever we're doing and run off to the woods for a week whenever we feel stressed.

That's why our larger goal is to learn how to stay centered and calm during those moments when life wants to throw you off balance, when everything is screaming for your attention and trying to upset you. These are going to be the moments when it's most important to learn to remain true to yourself: calm, focused, and centered. Learning to replace our less healthy reactions with an infinite patience is going to be the ultimate objective of any sort of meditation or self-focused conscious reflection. (Picture, if you will, the reserved dignity of Commander

Adama in the 2003-era update to the *Battlestar Galactica* franchise.)

Almost 2,000 years ago, the Greek philosopher Epictetus was talking about what we now call Emotional Intelligence. So why is this still a thing? Because it's really hard! Our brains are physically wired to feel before we think. (The neuron pathway to the frontal cortex first passes through the limbic system.) So learning to engage our rational mind and change our responses to frustration and perceived provocation, is not intuitive. It takes practice. On top of that, many of us don't even start trying to figure this out until later in life, so we've got decades of habit to unlearn. Which is why I'm in favor of teaching "social emotional learning" in schools. Whether we call it mindfulness, or EQ, or Emotional Awareness, this is a life skill that can make a difference.

There are many books, course, and apps on the subject. See, for example, the Insight Timer app, and the book *Emotional Intelligence 2.0* by Travis Bradberry and Jean Greaves.

Learning contentment, gratitude, and appreciation for the present moment: this is the path of ancient wisdom. As the *Tao Te Ching* teaches, "Those who know that enough is enough will always have enough."[18]

4.3 Catastrophizing

There is a difference between realism and pessimism.

Too often, what we call "realism" is in truth the lowest form of cynicism.

We all sometimes assume the worst, or predict bad outcomes; but if we are to enjoy a sunny day, we must break the habit of looking for storms when all is clear. When we are filled with worry and fear, then we are unable to enjoy the present moment.

In order to pursue our purpose to its fullest expression, we must remain open to opportunities as they arise: opportunities to build on goodness with more goodness, to make connections, and to develop ideas.

But excessive fearfulness may cause us to lose an opportunity.

Therefore, we must be aware of our tendency to engage in catastrophic thinking or "doom forecasting."

One time my sister was out of contact for a few weeks while she was traveling. It was a

---

18 Chapter 46

longer break in communications than usual, and it was just before I was due to fly over to the other side of the world and meet her there; so it was alarming that she hadn't been in touch to make arrangements. My Mom and I talked it over until we had convinced each other that something truly terrible must have befallen my sister. But by the time I reached my flight's layover, Lindsey had finally checked in. She said that there was limited connectivity where she was staying, and all the networks had been down. (This was in 2002, and she was in a very remote part of India at the time.) The point is, she was fine; and all of our worry and fear for her safety, was energy wasted. Worrying didn't improve the outcome, and only served to stress us out.

So when you feel yourself going gloom and doom, and predicting the worst, just remember, everything is probably going to be fine; and even if it's not, stressing out about it won't make anything better, anyway: so you may as well forget about your worries for the time being, and enjoy the present moment!

There's a very old saying:

"Now let us eat, drink, and be merry; for tomorrow, we may die!"

This sentiment is clearly expressed in *The Bible*:

"Then I commended mirth, because a man hath no better thing under the sun, than to eat, and to drink, and to be merry: for that shall abide with him of his labour the days of his life, which God giveth him under the sun." (Ecclesiastes 8:15)

But the ancient Hebrews were not the only ones who were thinking along these lines.

The ancient Egyptians offered similar advice:

"If you are brave, master your heart,
    and you will fill your embrace with your children,
  kiss your wife, and see your house!
  This is better than anything."[19]

The sentiment is perhaps best expressed in *The Epic of Gilgamesh*, a Sumerian myth

---

19 From "The Tale of the Shipwrecked Sailor," author unknown, preserved in the ancient manuscripts collectively known as the "Coffin Texts." This poem was probably composed in the early Twelfth Dynasty, during Egypt's Middle Kingdom (say, circa 1918 BCE or so): in other words, nearly **four thousand years ago**. Translated by R.B. Parkinson.

inscribed on clay tablets some four thousand years ago:

> "All humans are fated to die. Therefore, until your time arrives, enjoy your life! Spend your days in happiness, not despair. Each day, wash your head, bathe your body, and wear clothes that are sparkling fresh. Fill your stomach with tasty food. Play, sing, dance, and be happy both day and night. Delight in the pleasures of the marriage bed, and cherish the little child who holds your hand. **Make every day of your life a feast of rejoicing!** This is the task that the gods have set before all human beings. This is the life you should seek, for this is the best life a mortal can hope to achieve."[20]

Perhaps this Sumerian myth may have influenced the Jewish book of Kohelet, known in the Old Testament as Ecclesiastes. In addition to the passage quoted above, the same book advises the reader,

---

20 From *The Epic of Gilgamesh*, of one of the oldest surviving literary works ever created by humans. Emphasis added. The slight paraphrase presented here is mostly based on Chapter 6 of the translation by Donna Rosenberg, advised by Book X of the Stephen Mitchell translation.

"There is nothing better for a man, than that he should eat and drink, and that he should make his soul enjoy good in his labour. This also I saw, that it was from the hand of God." (Ecclesiastes 2:24, KJV)

These are not new ideas: it is the most ancient wisdom. I suspect, if we were to carefully peruse the ancient myths and poetry of China, Persia, Mali, the Mayans, and others, that we would find echoes of these same sentiments expressed by human beings all around the world and throughout time.

Today is a good day to heed the advice of the ancients.

Enjoy your life. Start today.

4.3.1 Loving Life: A Personal Perspective

My friend Vicki J. "Joy-Kindler" O'Grady-Longo, when she read my draft of this book, kindly suggested that I offer some examples at this point, demonstrating how I have followed through on my own choice to enjoy life more.

This first example may seem trivial on the surface, but in a deeper sense it connects with the very core of my Nature-loving being. Since I re-emerged from my own personal rock bottom, I have taken my kids camping a number of times. For various reasons, when my kids were younger, it was difficult for me to imagine taking them camping all by myself. But after I resurfaced from rock bottom, I cast all such objections aside. I took the initiative, and I made those camping trips happen. It sounds like a small thing: but this is deeply meaningful to me. I love camping and the great outdoors, and I love having the opportunity to share these experiences with my children.

Another example involves both travel and the practice of getting in touch with what we really want. My wife and I have been known to make detailed plans for our family vacations, filling every day with a schedule of activities. But after I participated in Mark Cumicek's dream challenge, I realized that what I really want to do is sit on the beach and relax. So when we planned our vacation to Mexico in early 2024, Jessica and I blocked out several days with no itinerary other than sitting on the beach; and that has been the highlight of my year so far.

That same dream challenge also raised for me the idea that I have always had an interest in making movies, but (other than a few dozen mostly-self-help videos on YouTube) I have not pursued that interest as an adult. As soon as this thought occurred, though, I reached out to Phillip Wade, who I had met through a local business networking group some eight or more years previously. I asked Phillip if he was still making movies, and a week later I found myself working behind the scenes on the production of his awesome science fiction movie, *Life Cycle 63*. That experience was so inspirational that now as I write this I'm currently working on organizing the production of my own first proper movie short. Once you get started on your path, you want to keep going!

And there is so much more. Within a period of about six months I ran my first half-marathon, worked on a movie crew, traveled abroad, and released a new album of music. I'm living the dream!

And I truly believe that you can live your dream, too.

I believe I can predict the most common objection to my optimism. Yes, it's true: it may take you several years to figure out the money problem. That was certainly true in my family, and we still have room for improvement. But you can do this! Talk with an accountant, if it would help; or better yet, take some accounting and business management classes. Look into loan forgiveness options, especially for student loans; and watch for opportunities to refinance high-interest loans at a lower rate. Generally prefer buy-and-hold investments to short-term flips or day trading. Long-term strategic planning may not seem very sexy, but it makes a hot difference in the long term.

Of course, turning these kinds of opportunities from idea to reality is not always easy. When you look at celebrity successes, remember: The trade-offs don't make the headlines. As an example from my own life, in the case of that album of music I just mentioned, what I didn't mention is, that album had taken me *six years* to complete! (I initially began recording it, but then abandoned it, during my "rock bottom" days.) But with dedication and determination we can achieve our goals. And most importantly, we can have fun doing it!

The above examples are not specific to eating and drinking; but they have certainly involved much merriment. I hope you can see how, when we decide to get more enjoyment out of life, we are able to follow through and find ways to enjoy life more.

Ask for what you want, my friends, in every area of your life: professionally, recreationally, and (although it's not the primary subject of this book, it's worth mentioning) even in the bedroom.

Ask for what you want! Your life will be more joyful and fulfilling as a result.

Start today!

4.3.2 Living with Purpose

Although I truly believe that the enjoyment of the present moment is the key to a more fulfilling life, this is not a call to reckless hedonic abandon. We must seek balance. Living without *any* care for the future will lead us into disaster rather quickly. As a reasonable, forward-thinking individual, you know that in order to truly, fully enjoy your life, you must plan for the future.

And if you reach a point in your life when you feel like there must be something more, or the simple pleasures of life do not seem to be quite enough for you: then you'll be ready to talk about purpose.

This notion of "purpose" is akin to the concept known as *dharma*, or right action, in the Eastern philosophies of Buddhism and Hinduism. It is that which we are meant to do. It doesn't look the same for everyone. It may change over time. But the clearest path to following your purpose is when you live in accordance with your core values.

It's not always easy to put your purpose into words. But you can sometimes feel it in your gut: either the sense of rightness when you're living in accordance with your purpose, or else the sense of emptiness when you've grown distracted from your purpose by the countless pressures of life.

Do what you enjoy doing. Do what you feel you were meant to do. Make choices that bring your life and actions into accordance with your core values. Follow your purpose, and follow your dreams.

You can do amazing things. You can find your passion and pursue your purpose. May you feel fulfilled.

4.4 Projection

We often *believe* that we understand other people, much better than we *actually* understand other people. It's a very human tendency. We think we know what someone else is thinking. We credit ourselves with extraordinary capabilities.

This is an example of a psychological phenomenon called **projection**.

As often happens with words, this one may mean something different to different people.

To some, "projection" specifically refers to our explanations for other people's *deeds*. By this definition, projection occurs when we imply a motive for another person's actions (for example, "They said that because they wanted to upset me").[21] While that's a valid example, I believe the definition is much too narrow.

Projection occurs whenever we imagine that someone else's mind contains certain thoughts. We are making the assumption that the other person is thinking the thoughts that we ourselves have imagined for them.

Projection is an assumption. It's often incorrect; and it's often not very charitable.

When we imagine that we know what others are thinking, we are most often projecting our own **fears and insecurities**.

When we engage in projection, we make assumptions: and assumptions are frequently incorrect. We often make invalid, false assumptions when we engage in projection.

---

21 Assumptions about another's *intent* is projection. Drawing inferences about another's *character* is the Fundamental Attribution Error. We'll come back to this later.

When we project, we are projecting our own thoughts onto our perceptions of other people.

The thoughts don't belong to the other person. They are our thoughts. We are the ones who are thinking those thoughts which we attribute to others! We're not actually mind readers. We don't know what other people are thinking. It's not possible to know! We can make assumptions; and yes, sometimes our assumptions may be correct. But a few instances of being wrong can be disastrous.

We all sometimes fall into the trap of believing that we know what other people are thinking; but what we imagine inside the other person's mind is actually a reflection of our own thoughts and assumptions. When we remember this, we can remain more open to true communication and connection in the moment.

4.4.1 Introjection

Introjection is the reverse of projection. This occurs when another person's thoughts are injected into our own minds.

For example, another person's comments, whether offhand or calculated, overt or implied, can sometimes become wedged in our own thoughts. Then these thoughts swirl around and around. We may sometimes hold onto and repeat them to ourselves until they sound like our own thoughts.

Someone else has placed a thought in your mind at some time in your life. You probably know who they were, and no fancy *Inception* technology was required. They simply spoke, and the thought was planted.

Unfortunately, introjection is most likely to occur with the sort of cruel, judgmental, derogatory remarks that tend to undermine our self-confidence.

As Daniel Amen points out in *Change Your Brain, Change Your Life*, the people around us feed our thinking. That's why it's very important to choose the people we spend our time with: because if they are people who embrace the power of the positive, then they can feed our positive thoughts; whereas if they are constantly spewing negativity, then they will most certainly feed our negative thoughts.

If we want to choose to have more positive thoughts in the future, then we must carefully safeguard which thoughts we allow others to put into our minds.

4.4.2 Deflection

Another concept worth remembering here is deflection.

We engage in deflection when we respond to criticism by leveling an accusation against someone else.

We may not even be aware that we are doing this. In the example of deflection offered by Jordan B. Petersen, we might say, "I'm not sensitive, it's just that you're really annoying." But if we are too emotionally invested in diverting criticism, at some point we begin shirking our responsibilities; and that's not who we want to be. We want to be people of integrity; and people of integrity accept criticism.

Another form of deflection is to avoid direct questions by turning the question around on the other person. For example, when asked, "Did you steal the item you're holding right now?" a thief might reply, "Did *you* steal the item I'm holding right now?" It's a device employed for comic effect in television shows like *Dirk Gently's Holistic Detective Agency*, but it's both maddening and really suspiciously evasive when someone pulls this in real life.

So don't be like that.

Instead, be direct with people.

Be truthful, but maintain boundaries. Avoid going to extremes and spilling your guts to random strangers. Let us seek balance, and live with integrity.

4.5 Understanding the Negativity Bias

We learn through repetition. When neurons make connections with each other, the brain reinforces the physical pathway between those neurons. When we make certain mental associations repeatedly over time, those brain connections are strengthened to the point where they become habits or even dominant personality traits.

On the other hand, when connections in the brain are neglected, they weaken over time, dissipate, and are replaced. Thus an athlete or musician must constantly practice, or they will begin to lose their edge.

The more we do certain things, the more we think certain ways, the stronger those associated neural pathways become.

That's part of the reason why it's so important to consciously focus on the positive.

Conversely, when we dwell on negative thoughts, that negativity seeps out from our mind into the real world, and can have a detrimental impact on every area of our lives.

But when we intentionally redirect and focus our thoughts on joy, on love, on our purpose and our values: then we strengthen our positive mental connections, and those *positive* impacts seep into every aspects of our lives, and infuse every moment with joy.

Can you feel it? Can you feel the love and joy, inviting you to join your soul in a wonderful sense of wholeness?

Perhaps not yet. You have a lot to overcome, plus some limiting factors that are innate to every human being.

One of those limiting factors is called the negativity bias. This is a natural phenomenon that causes the human brain to notice and remember negative information (for example, information that is frightening, disgusting, or upsetting) more readily than it grasps onto other types of information.

As has been discussed by many writers, the negativity bias evolved because it provides an evolutionary benefit in one sense, helping our ancestors to remember to run from saber-toothed tigers; but it can be situationally maladaptive in a modern context.

As human beings, we take negative information more seriously, we remember it longer, and we recall it more readily. This is how our brains have evolved. Our negative experiences and memories may become so deeply ingrained by this mechanism that they become an inseparable part of who we are, the core of our identities, whereas our more positive experiences and memories may simply dissipate and wash away. According to Shawn Achor in *Before Happiness*, a single piece of negative information has more impact on the brain than many pieces of positive information. Therefore, the mind would require many, many positive inputs to counterbalance a single negative input. If we've experienced something negative in the past, we should be going out of our way to continuously surround ourselves with positive symbols and messages in the present to help us consciously shape our narrative going into the future.

But what do we do instead? You know the answer! We immerse ourselves in negative messages via the news, and social media, and our info-tainment. We surround ourselves with constant negativity. On some level, negativity is like junk food, or crack cocaine: we may even recognize that it's bad for us, but we begin to crave it. It's an easy way to get a rush.

Wholesome ideas, by way of contrast, may initially seem like hard work.

For example, cleaning is harder than destroying. It's easy to make a mess: you can even do it instantly, by accident. Cleaning, on the other hand, requires decisive action, a certain amount of forethought, the dedication of time and effort, and often some tools and supplies, and sometimes you get messy in the process, or sometimes you may have to contort yourself to reach inside an awkward space. So when you decide to clean, it's not because cleaning is inherently fun (although there are ways to make anything more fun, if you want to) but because afterwards we feel better about ourselves and about our lives. A clean, well-organized space gives the mind the freedom to express itself without frequently encountering clutter. (I say this, and yet there is clutter on my desk where I am typing this, so I certainly have room for improvement in this respect myself.) That's why Paul McCartney once wrote a song about performing routine home maintenance tasks, like fixing a hole in his roof, and filling in the cracks in his walls: because those signs of disrepair had interrupted his thoughts in the free pursuit of their natural wanderings. And, he concluded in the same song, in the end it's not important who's right and who's wrong. Perhaps it's time to revisit Marie Kondo after all.

Take charge of your life. Start with the things you can control: your thoughts, your personal space, your actions and words, your part of your relationships with other people. Be aware of the sentiments you express and how those thoughts impact those around you. Be aware of the sentiments expressed by those around you as well, and notice how they impact you. In addition to the actual people around you, this also includes the books, magazines, blogs, feeds, and other things you read; as well as the various movies, shows, broadcasts, and other screen and multimedia content you consume. For each item, ask yourself: What kind of thoughts is this putting in your head? Does it fill you with love? Or does it fill you with... the opposite of love?

4.6   Love and Its Opposite: An Analytical Framework

It felt like a tremendous breakthrough in my own personal journey when I realized that all people experience emotions and engage in behaviors which we can easily classify as expressions of either love, or hate.

Many readers will consider this analytical framework overly simplistic or even reductive, and that's fine. I'm not saying you have to live by this distinction forever. Just try it out as a thought exercise for the purpose of this argument, and see where the thought takes you.

4.6.1 Love.

In this thought exercise, some examples of love might include such positive emotions and behaviors as joy, gratitude, hope, confidence, warmth, acceptance, friendliness, inclusion, compassion, dignity, respect, tolerance, understanding, empathy, forgiveness, humility, listening, helping, generosity, kindness, patience, balance, integrity, justice, truth, freedom, equanimity, learning, encouragement, awareness, gratitude, faith, wonder, awe, kindness, charity, grace, trust, peace, happiness, bliss, and contentment.

You can love yourself, and you can love others. In this view, self-confidence and self-respect may be seen as love for oneself. Far from being "narcissistic," **loving oneself turns out to be absolutely, fundamentally**

essential to your survival. If you don't love yourself right now, I hope you will learn to love yourself soon: because you are worthy of love. Yes, you. You are worthy of love. Believe it. Don't forget it. And don't let anybody tell you otherwise.

In order to lead a meaningful life, we must fill our hearts with love, devote our thoughts to goodness, and pursue a sense of purpose in accordance with our values. In order to better connect to the Universe and to our fellow human beings, we must understand and contemplate love: especially selfless love, interpersonal connection, and universal tolerance.

The greatest goal in life, is to experience more love. Often, we get love by giving love. It's not a transaction: it's an instinctive reaction. When we're in a good frame of mind, it's self-reinforcing. The people around us see us exude positive emotions, and they respond by feeding us their own positive emotions, which makes us feel good, which makes us exhibit positive behaviors, which makes the people around us respond in kind, and so on.

Love is not merely limited to romance or family ties. Love can be the ability to see others as unique individuals who are presently at this particular point in their life journey, just as you yourself are presently at this particular point in your own life journey. You're journeying together through this is a life, and this journey will take you far, because you're going to start today.

4.6.2 The Other Thing

Well, if that's love, in this thought exercise, then obviously hate is all the other stuff.

And as uncomfortable as this may be, we must learn to understand the opposite of love, that we may better recognize it when we see it, and choose to avoid not only that path but also the thoughts that tend to lead us there.

So allow yourself to pause and consider this for a moment; and if not at this moment, then perhaps consider this at a later moment when you have the time and mental space to address a complicated idea. And when you're ready, think about this:

Some expressions of hate might include blame, guilt, shame, judgment, denunciation, and condemnation; hypocrisy, malice, spite, vindictiveness, vengeance, and revenge; mockery, stereotyping, discrimination, exclusion, excommunication, and ostracism;

superiority, inferiority, envy, enmity, gossip, name-calling, fear, and of course, contempt.

And the key insight here is that we *all* engage in these negative emotions sometimes. Yes, all of us! It's not just *them*, and it's certainly not just you: it's all of us. Hate is far more common than most people are willing to admit these days.

Oh, I know, most of us recoil from the word "hate." We would never admit that we harbor such terrible feelings. Hate is something that only our enemies do, right? Our enemies (whoever they may be) are defined by their hate; and we by contrast are defined by our moral superiority: our claim of being "better than them." In fact, we believe that it is precisely this act of judging our enemies for their flaws which makes us "better than them." In this way, we incite hatred against our political opponents by accusing our opponents of harboring hatred.

But all this is a logical fallacy.

Judging others is a form of hate! And yet, we all do it sometimes. So let us not be so quick to condemn others for experiencing human emotions of their own.

If we're to be people of integrity, then we must become aware of our own faults and flaws. If one of our flaws is that we sometimes indulge maleficent thoughts, it's much healthier to admit this to ourselves, than to deny it.

We must acknowledge the depth of our feelings; and then we must do our best to release them. When we learn to recognize this emotion for what it is, then we may consciously choose to move on to a more positive mindset, and to focus our thoughts on our gratitude in the present moment.

We must come to terms with our emotion if we are to work through it and come out whole on the other side.

Avoiding or *suppressing* our negative emotion is not a workable solution. These things have a tendency to float to the surface. If we try to push it down, it's likely to pop back up with a vengeance later in a really ugly and unexpected way.

On the other hand, *dwelling* on our negative emotions will likewise create more of them, until we may begin to find ever-more devastating ways to express them.

Neither extended focus nor willful ignorance will make these feelings go away. We must acknowledge and understand our own feelings if we are to move past them and return to a state of equanimity and grace.

It may help to recall that our feelings are often a product of unrelated stressors.

In the political sphere, hate and fear are powerful motivators, and have been throughout history: with terrible consequences for us all.

No matter the setting, it is all too easy to demonize the target of one's hatred: to lose sight of what we share with them as a human being, and to believe all manner of untrue things about them. We see this in the news, and throughout human history: people who dwell on their feelings of hatred for too long, tend to act out in irrational and violent ways.

The solution to all this is an aspect of mindfulness.

We must be self-aware.

We must recognize our negative emotions for what they are, accept that we are experiencing them, try to understand what brought this moment about for us, and then set this moment aside and move on to the next moment by refocusing our attention on the positive, such as something we are grateful for. Focusing the mind on gratitude, thankfulness, and appreciation can help to redirect our energies back into a more positive sphere. I understand that when we are in the dark depths of bitterness and despair it can be difficult to focus the mind on gratitude, but it is always a worthwhile exercise, and like all exercises the more we practice the better at it we get.

We must avoid the easy habit of automatically judging others. We need to learn acceptance, tolerance, compassion, forgiveness, and love. These are the road to a better life.

We can get away from judging others by recognizing our own imperfections. I'm not perfect. You're not perfect. Ain't nobody perfect. And we have to learn to accept that. We all have faults, and we all make mistakes.

And yet, even as we contemplate our own flaws, we must be careful to consider this information with acceptance, and without judgment against ourselves. Our faults and flaws are elements of our humanity, and opportunities for improvement: nothing more. Your inner self is that glowing core, filled with a beauty that transcends all else. Our faults and flaws, whatever they may be, cannot mar the wholeness, purity, and perfection of our inner selves.

4.6.2.1 Blame

Many of us are very fond of blame. Blame offers the narrative that all our problems are someone else's fault. We learn to see ourselves as the innocent victim in a world of evil perpetrators.

Blame is socially acceptable, even encouraged, in our modern cultural environment. Many of our social relationships and even our cherished belief systems are deeply rooted in a sense of blame and its associated victimhood. We have come to cherish the blame itself. Our enemies become essential to our own identity: we define ourselves as being "better than" them. If it were to suddenly turn out that everyone is pretty much the same, and all people are merely people, everywhere and throughout time: then that would challenge our very notion of ourselves! We're prepared to fight that idea. We insist that blame couldn't possibly be a form of hate; because if that were true, then we would have to admit that we have wasted years of our lives spewing hatred on social media.

So let's start off with the assumption that, yes: You have wasted years of your life spewing hatred on social media, and so have I, and so have most of the people we know. (In the age of the algorithm, clicking the "like" button counts almost as if you posted it, so let's all take full responsibility for our actions.)

Most opinion pieces on most news websites contain elements of hate. In fact, most jokes contain elements of hate. Most Tweets are pure hate: *especially* those screenshots of Tweets that people post on other platforms.

Having recognized this, now we're going to try to move away from our own habitual thought-pattern of hate based on blame, and move into a new pattern based on acceptance.

We can't accept personal responsibility for our problems if we are simultaneously blaming all our problems on others who we label "toxic," or whatever the popular label is today. If we are to be great leaders, it is our responsibility to find the best in our team members: not to label and blame them. As Brené Brown reminds us, most people are usually doing their best.

And that goes for us. We're doing our best, too!

Blaming ourselves is no better than blaming others. Blame is a value judgment, and value judgments interfere with the process of acceptance and forgiveness which is required for healing.

Rather than falling down the hole of guilt, recriminations, and the blaming of the self or others, we must accept our present circumstances, and make choices in the present that will take us on the path to a better future.

Consider a worst-case scenario. If you are stuck in a truly hopeless situation, enslaved with no hope of escape by cruel barbarians who torture you: then you can still do your best to accept the present with serenity, until you find an opportunity to escape. Your situation is unjust, but it is not your fault.

Few of us find ourselves in such a position. But consider another worst-case scenario. Even if you are presently imprisoned – even if you were falsely convicted by a biased criminal justice system – you can still probably take this time to improve yourself with exercise and reading. Self-improvement is a better outlet than wallowing in guilt or despair or dreams of revenge. Accept the present circumstances, and find a path forward.

If you are neither imprisoned nor enslaved, think of how fortunate you are.

When I failed in my own life, the popular "blame your parents and society" type of world view had a strong appeal for me. It allowed me to tell myself that none of my problems were really my own fault. That allowed me to feel lots of **blame**; but it did not solve any of my problems. On the contrary: this world view left me feeling powerless!

The key to positive change is knowing – and believing – that there is something you can *do* to address your problems. When we see a path to a better future, we can take responsibility for walking that path. We gain agency over our own lives. We control our own destinies.

That's how I felt. Making any progress towards actually solving my problems required me to believe that I had the ability to change my own life; and it required me to develop the ability to choose how I look at the world, including the ability to tell myself a different kind of story about my own life. Meaningfully addressing my problems required me to reject the perspective of a world of oppression and hostility, and to choose instead to see a world filled with hope and opportunity.

It's a choice. Yeah, we've all been through some shit, but that was in the past. The future is up to you. You get to choose. What kind of person do you want to be?

I hope you'll choose to be awesome.

4.6.2.2 Judgment

Once you recognize judgment and blame as forms of hate, you begin to see things differently. We must be always evaluating our own actions to eliminate any hypocrisy.

Just try to feel at one with the world around you, at one with the present moment.

This moment is perfect, it is complete, it is unique, it is so brief that several moments passed during the time it took to read this sentence.

In this moment, you can set aside all worries and complaints and live as one with the world.

Moving beyond judgment and blame can be extremely difficult. They are habitual responses, socially reinforced. We tell ourselves that we *have* to judge and blame others for our own protection; and yet judgment and blame cause harm that spirals into escalating retaliation, bitterness, grudges, fear, and hate.

We want to succeed in our own goals without harming others. Judging others, perpetuating stereotypes, calling names, spreading rumors: these harm others. If we believe that we are all essentially the same, then we will not judge others so much, but rather we will say instead, "That person is a lot like me, and I am a lot like them, and all people are just people, no matter where you go, everywhere and throughout time."

If you are a reflection of myself, then how can I judge you? If I see you as embodying the same basic humanity that I feel within myself, then how can I judge you? If we are just two specks in a great Cosmic Oneness, interconnected on a quantum level by forces we can each barely begin to comprehend, then how can I judge you? Fundamentally, you are no better than me, and I am no better than you. We are equals, both deserving of love and decency and dignity and compassion and kindness and respect. Therefore, the key is we must treat one another as equals deserving of decency and dignity. If we feel we're not being treated with the dignity we deserve, it's up to us to stand up for ourselves and demand the treatment we deserve – without inflicting retaliatory damage against the other party.

Oh, it gets complex, and sometimes we must take strong measures to protect ourselves, because people are sometimes greedy, and the greedy sometimes employ deception; so no generalization can hold true at all times. But as a general guideline, one of the greatest precepts of all time is,

"Judge not, that ye be not judged.... First cast out the beam out of thine own eye; and then shalt thou see clearly to cast out the mote out of thy brother's eye." (Matt. 7:1-5)

Yes, you're allowed to notice that there's a mote in your brother's eye. If someone is causing trouble, you don't have to pretend to be oblivious to their bullshit. But when your own problem is bigger than your brother's problem, then you really have no business fuckin' with your brother's eyes. Leave him alone, and deal with your own shit first.

If you're feeling unfairly judged in your life right now, then you can immediately understand the value of the injunction to "judge not."

But if you're feeling unfairly *hurt* in your life right now, then you may be deeply attached to your feelings of blame. That's understandable, it's perfectly natural, and it's the emotional attachment from which we all must learn to let go.

We come back to it. The mind returns to the place of hurt due to association triggers and the negativity bias.

But we can learn to redirect the mind. We can correct for the negativity bias with intentionality. We can choose to focus on what is good.

We are fortunate to be alive. We are blessed to experience this moment. This moment is an opportunity to feel at one with the Cosmos, to be at peace with the world, to be in love with the Universe, and to feel the reciprocal Universal Love shining on you and shining within you. Breathe in, and resonate with the awareness that in this moment, you are breathing in. Breathe out, and allow your awareness to be completely filled with the experience of breathing out in this precious moment. The focus on the breath is central to many meditation practices, including the teachings of Thich Nhat Hanh.

It is hard to let go of blame. (Carl Alasko wrote a whole book on the subject, titled *Beyond Blame*.) Someone has hurt you, and it was unfair! You feel what you feel. We accept the validity of your feelings.

But holding onto it will keep the pain alive for you. It keeps the trauma fresh. It prevents the past from receding into the past. It is the thought-pain which the Buddhists describe as the "second arrow," the mental anguish caused by *thinking* about the injury. You know the feeling when a bad feeling, memory, or thought recurs repeatedly, distracting us from the present moment and keeping us locked in a negative spiral. It's like the mind gets stuck replaying some painful experience from the past on a loop. We experience the pain over and over as the mind replays these thoughts and memories. The first arrow is the initial injury, and the second arrow is only in our mind; but it is the second arrow that hurts worse.

When we get caught up in stressful feelings of blame and shame, regardless of whether those feelings are directed inwards or outwards (or, as is so often the case, both) then sometimes the anger and hurt may take hold of our awareness and won't let go. Eventually, we carry that pain around with us in every present moment of our daily lives, and then our pain from the past begins to interfere with our interactions and break down our relationships in the present.

We wish to experience a life of joy and happiness, free from pain and anxiety to the greatest extent possible. Therefore, we must learn to relinquish our hold on our painful thoughts, and instead focus on gratitude and the present moment.

There is much to be grateful for. For myself, I have the opportunity to sit outdoors as I write this. The air is fresh. I am hydrated and well-nourished. I live in a beautiful place, where I have the opportunity to enjoy nature. I live at a unique time in human history, when social and technological change are both occurring at a momentous pace. There is much to appreciate.

Have gratitude for all that has gone well in your life, and all the fortune you have, right now. Yes, right now. If you really, really can't think of anything to be grateful for right now, wonder at something outside yourself. How wonderful that you have air to breathe. If you are reading this, marvel at the fact that you have eyes to see with, and allow yourself to be amazed at all there is to see in this wide world. If you are listening to these words, marvel at the fact that you have ears to hear, and the capacity for understanding. Still not feeling grateful? Well, look at it this way: If you are not in prison right now, then no matter what else is bad in your life, you can be grateful that at least you're not in prison. And if you are in prison right now, then you can take pride in the fact that you are making the effort to transform your mindset while you're inside, no matter what circumstances landed you there. Whoever you are, you've been doing the best you could in life, given the circumstances and the experiences and the beliefs you've had up to this point. You're reading this because you see room for improvement in your life. And that tells me that you're the kind of person who can find the motivation to make a change. I believe you will emerge a better person because of the work you're doing on yourself right now. Now it's time for you to believe in yourself.

Surround yourself with positive messages.

If your mind rebels against positive messages, it's usually for one of two primary reasons: either the messages themselves are fundamentally cynical or hypocritical, and they only *appear* positive on the surface; or else your mind has become so accustomed to cynical thinking, that it automatically rejects truly positive messages. The good news is, if it's the latter, you can change your thinking; and if it's the former, then you don't have to.

So surround yourself with positive messages. Surround yourself with positive images. Surround yourself with positive people.

Let the positivity wash over you and flow through you. Absorb it until you yourself begin to exude positivity.

Learn from everyone around you, but always choose your own way.

Set the standard. Be the example. Show everyone else the way. Let your inner light be their guiding star.

Of course, as soon as I say that, I become instantly aware of my own failings and imperfections. Who am I to be an example? The answer is, I'm not an example of perfection: because nobody is perfect. Instead, I'm an example of someone who keeps trying. So keep trying. We're all just human. Do the best you can do, and don't be overly harsh in your self-criticism if the end product is somehow different from some of your earliest grand visions. If it's important enough, you can learn from this experience and use that knowledge to do better next time.

Remember that, as Brené Brown tells us, most people are usually doing the best they can.[22]

That's a big thought, isn't it?

Most people are usually doing the best they can.

---

22 Although the saying has certainly been popularized by Brown, a similar quote is credited to Deepak Chopra. I don't know who really said it first; probably neither of them. Based on quick search results, this concept has been a subject of discussion within psychology circles for at least a dozen years, and possibly quite a bit longer.

We find that hard to accept: because we can all think of someone who is doing pretty poorly! But that's our tendency to judge. If we can accept others as they are, maybe we can learn to work with them, instead.

There's another key principle that comes into play here, which it's helpful to understand: and that's the Fundamental Attribution Error.

4.7 The Fundamental Attribution Error

When someone else makes a mistake or commits an infraction, we tend to perceive the misdeed as a reflection of that individual's character. For example, we might say, "That person is a bad driver *because* they are a bad person."

By way of contrast, when we ourselves make a mistake or commit an infraction, we become lawyers: recognizing complexity, nuance, extenuating circumstances, loopholes, provisos, and the broken system that left us with no visible choices. We apply different standards when judging others than the standards we use to judge ourselves. For example, we might tell ourselves, "I'm not really a bad driver, but I *had to* break the speed limit, because I was running late for an appointment, and it was really important, because blah blah blah."[23]

Looking beyond the driving example, we see that in fact complexity, nuance, and extenuating circumstances often *do* have some legitimate validity; and if we're not judging others, then there's no sense in evaluating the matter further.

In fact, all manner of accidents, mistakes, misjudgments, errors, and even criminal behavior can be largely prevented or significantly decreased through systems transformation, process improvements, and large-scale programs. It's a central premise of the book *Switch: How to Change Things when Changing Things is Hard* by Chip Heath and Dan Heath.

So for those of us who are interested in management, leadership, and systems analysis, we should strive to implement systems transformation when it's feasible.

And at the same time, on an individual level, no matter who we are, if we want to take control of our own lives, we can't just sit around blaming

---

23 Unfortunately, that kind of excuse makes all the other excuses look bad. It sounds better to simply own it and say, "I broke the speed limit because I enjoy the feeling of driving fast." (Please, drive safely and responsibly. At this writing I think it's been at least five years since my last speeding ticket.)

the system: we have to do what we can with what we have, in the present.

4.8 Victim Mentality

"I don't have a victim mentality!" the mind protests. "It's just that the world is so unfair!"

Sometimes we get so caught up in our thoughts about the harm we have suffered from other people that we lose any sense of agency over our own lives.

We may become trapped by our trauma in a state of learned helplessness in which we begin to believe that we are powerless to improve our situation. We may become so fully immersed in our victim narrative that the victimhood begins to form the core of our identity or even our ideology. The hurt and the blame become all-consuming.

When we are consumed by hurt and blame, we get lost in negative cycles. Sometimes we are so filled with negativity that we actively provoke others, and they predictably respond by lashing out, which reinforces our self-image of victimhood. We even begin to mock and deride the very idea of hope itself as an unrealistic dream.

But that's no way to live! There is always hope.

Once you lose sight of hope, it's easy to become overwhelmed by a concept of yourself as a powerless victim.

But it's time to claim your power.

It's time to tell yourself a story of your life in which you are not a victim anymore. It's time to tell yourself a narrative that there is something you can do to change your circumstances, that you will be able to take control of your own life and drive positive change.

In our minds, we all tell ourselves stories about our lives. In down moments, our mental stories tend to be an endless complaint about all the people who have wronged us, and everything that's preventing us from moving on, as well as self-recrimination for all our own mistakes and problems and personal foibles that we believe will become an insurmountable future obstacle. But that's not helpful. None of that is helpful.

If you spend all your mental effort memorizing a list of injuries you have suffered and reasons why you can't succeed, then it's going to be a hell of a lot more difficult for you to succeed!

Focus instead on all the ways in which you *will* succeed!

Redirect your thoughts to gratitude for the beauty of Nature and all that has gone well in your life.

And when your thoughts wander the wrong way again, as they most assuredly will, you can focus and redirect them back to positivity again.

Do you want to change your life? Are you stuck in a shitty situation and you want out? The first step, the most important step, is for you to **believe** that change is possible.

Personal transformation begins with mindset. Changing your life demands action. The mindset inspires the action. And successful action reinforces the mindset.

Mindset change makes life change possible.

Believe in possibilities.

4.8.1 The Victim Triangle

Before we move on, there's one more aspect of the victim mentality that we must consider, and that concerns interpersonal interactions.

I'm aware of two different models of the Victim Triangle, and they are both illuminating as models of problematic interpersonal interactions.

The model of the Victim Triangle which I encountered first is that described by Dr. Michael Pariser in his book, *No More Mr. Nice Guy: The Hero's Journey* (a companion workbook, not to be confused with the original *No More Mr. Nice Guy* by Dr. Robert Glover).

In his book, Dr. Pariser describes our desire to be seen as the Rescuer. We swoop in to try to help the Victim, who tells us about the awful Perpetrator in their life and/or in their past. At first, we're certain we can make everything better. But the more deeply we become involved in the Victim's life drama, the more we come to realize that nothing is going to save this person until they deal with their own deep-rooted personal issues. Meanwhile the Victim begins to resent us, because we've been ineffective as Rescuers; and as that resentment builds, the Victim may eventually begin to accuse us of being just another Perpetrator. Faced with such unfair accusations, we adopt the mentality of the Victim ourselves; and from there, things go downhill fast.

Some time later, I discovered there's another way of viewing the same dynamic.

In *The Coaching Habit*, Michael Bungay Stanier discusses what he calls the Karpman

Drama Triangle, as developed by Dr. Stephen Karpman.

In the Karpman model of the Victim Triangle, each of us plays all three roles: Victim, Persecutor, and Rescuer. In this model, we may frequently switch between all three of these roles, sometimes several times within a single brief interaction. When we're upset with others who we feel aren't doing their fair share, for example, then we become the Persecutor. When others retort, or attack us in retaliation for perceived slights, we become the Victim. And when others complain about how unfair it all is, we play the role of the Rescuer. But a Rescuer is easily seen as a Persecutor, and our attempts to act as the Rescuer either reinforces or triggers Victim behavior in the other person.

It's best not to play any of these three roles. Since the roles are to some extent inevitable (these are archetypical human traits, after all) we must be aware of our own tendencies and behaviors, and how those impact others, so that we may maintain our equanimity, and mitigate these negative effects as best we can.

4.9 The Need to Be Right

As long as the human mind has been capable of forming judgments, humans have been judging one another. From the prehistoric caves of our distant ancestors to the social media forums of today, being judged too harshly may have dire consequences for our lives. If we are seen as "wrong" then we might be seen as "bad;" and if we are seen as "bad" then we might be socially isolated or ostracized by the group. If we are socially isolated or ostracized, then not only do we face diminished access to resources and opportunity, we are also threatened by greater exposure to a variety of dangers: from wild animals and the ancient elements, to organized rings of modern cyber criminals. Prolonged social isolation is psychologically strenuous for the human animal (and in some instances may provoke harmful behavior). Therefore, being seen as "wrong" is so dangerous that it may prove fatal; and in order to avoid this, we have been conditioned with a deeply ingrained, almost instinctive drive to be seen as right; or at least, to avoid being seen as wrong.

Being seen as "right" thus becomes a survival behavior driven by primal fear. And the easiest way to be seen as right, is to make *someone else* look wrong! (Witness modern politics.)

To this end, we go out of our way to prove others wrong, so that we may bask in the reflected glory of being right. We argue with whoever happens to be there, desperate to prove ourselves right. We argue, and argue, and argue, until we have pissed off all our friends and nobody wants to be around us.

As Eckhart Tolle among others has pointed out, the "need to be right" is a function of fear. We believe that our rightness is what makes us good; their wrongness is what makes our enemies bad: and being more right than them is what makes us superior.

We rationalize our obsession with proving others wrong by explaining that other people's false assumptions and wrong-headed beliefs may have negative consequences: so (we claim) we are the good guys, because we want to correct them! But in fact, if we're frequently arguing over trivialities and assumptions, this is a display of our own insecurities. We're desperate to prove that we're right, because deep down we are filled with fear that others might see us as wrong. We subconsciously counter this fear with an act of deflection. We go out of our way to prove that others are wrong.

And of course when we focus too much of our mental energy on thoughts about how wrong everyone else is, it stokes our sense of grievance and feeds a victim mentality. And victim mentality sometimes convinces people that they're justified in doing horrible things.

During my recent adventures in politics, it was clear that *everyone* on both sides is extremely convinced that they are very right about everything, and that the other side is so completely wrong as to be utterly evil! Meh. I'm pragmatic enough to know better. Oh, yeah, sure, sometimes when I get up in my feels I still want to prove how right I am! But when I step back, I see that sometimes my side is wrong, and sometimes the other side is right; and vice versa: and basically we're all just human, trying to do the best we can. I would ask you to question your assumptions, my friends. We're often quick to judge and slow to reconsider: but the path to Universal Love is non-judgmental.

4.10 Ego versus Greatness

We're often told to disregard the ego, as if the ego were the source of all evil.

I figure, as soon as people go around saying that *anything* is "the source of all evil," then whatever they're pointing fingers at, is probably misunderstood.

So let's take a moment to better understand the ego.

The ego is the voice of want.

Like many of the concepts discussed in this chapter, the ego serves an evolutionary purpose.

Without the ego, we would sit around in mindless contentment, never eating, never reproducing, never protecting ourselves from danger. Perhaps such a desireless and carefree existence might be somewhat pleasant, briefly; and then we would die, painfully, leaving no offspring. Thank goodness our ancestors had egos! We are alive today only because our ancestors felt driven by their egos to do, to make, to attain, to achieve, to become.

But on the other hand, the ego can be deeply problematic, because "want" can never be satisfied. As soon as we get something, we want more, or we want something else. We want pleasure, we want love, we want respect, we want *things*; we want our high standards and expectations to be met, all the time; we want property, we want status, we want power. We want to feel important. Often, when we find (inevitably) that we can't have what we want, or when we feel that we have received injuries instead: then we give way to emotion, and our most destructive tendencies are unleashed.

This is why so many teach that the ego is the source of all our problems.

But I dare to disagree. I believe that the ego can *also* be the very source of human greatness.

Whatever we achieve in life, whatever we are driven to do, whatever purpose we pursue with every fiber of our being: that, too, is a manifestation of the ego. The ego makes greatness possible: and greatness is the stuff of legend.

Even as some factions of our society adopt increasingly hostile and derogatory attitudes towards anyone who has attained any sort of greatness in our world: even now, *greatness itself* continues to be celebrated by our culture. Even though we occasionally demote some old figures and elevate new figures in their place, greatness itself retains its exalted position. No amount of social upheaval will ever remove this fundamental dynamic, nor should we want it to. Instead, let us each aspire to greatness in our own way.

True greatness, like enlightenment, may be illusory and subjective. For example, I felt brief transcendent moments of what I experienced as true greatness when playing with my rock band, which broke up more than a dozen years ago: the lineup we called Operation J, with the great Tom "The Count" Morgan on drums, "Screemin" Steve Hovey on bass, and the inimitable Andy "Androcles" Hoke on the keyboards. As a band, we were never "great" in terms of being famous or anything like that; but I personally believe we achieved moments of "greatness" during our rehearsals and rare public performances, when the music attained a sort of metaphysical transcendence. Even if it was only momentary, in those moments I felt that we were truly great.

And those are the sorts of moments of greatness that anyone can achieve, if we allow ourselves to strive for greatness.

So don't be ashamed of your ego. Don't suppress it, but instead, direct it. Don't reject the ego, because that's like rejecting your own hands; and don't try to drown out its voice, because that's an exercise in futility. Instead, accept the ego as a part of yourself, and learn to use it to your advantage, in harmonious concert with the egos of those around you.

There's nothing wrong with pursuing your purpose. Just choose a suitably worthy purpose, and fucking go for it.

Start today.

Part 5: Finish Strong and Start Again

There is so much more to say! There is always more to do. There are so many great ideas to think about. There are so many great books to discuss.

But this book is called *Start Today*. It's not intended to walk you through every step of your journey. This book is only meant to help you get started.

Pick yourself up off the floor, if that's where you are now. Choose to take responsibility for your future. Make some big decisions, and put one foot in front of the other. Before you know it, you will have made tremendous progress!

And when, inevitably, your initial burst of motivation starts to run down, or you hit a complication or a setback, or you find old mental patterns reasserting themselves: then it will be time to revisit this book; or to read some of my sources, which I highly recommend (they're listed at the end); or to digest some of the many other excellent resources available to students and practitioners of the self-help philosophy.

But all that happens later.

Right now, all you've got to do is start. Take that step: the first step of your thousand mile journey. Plant that tree: since you didn't plant it decades ago, plant it now!

Start today.

5.1 It's a process

Changing your life is not something you just do once and then you're done. Changing your life is a process of becoming; and the deeper the change, the more far-reaching its effects on every aspect of your life.

Changing your life is not confined to working hours; it is not confined to a specific location; it continues even when you take a vacation or go on a date. That's not to say you will start being some kind of "workaholic." We're seeking *balance* here. Ideally you'll find the fabled way to increase your income while decreasing your working hours. The point is that your life is everywhere you go and everything you do; and when your life changes, everything around you changes, too. A lot of that is because you begin to see it differently; but part of that is because people recognize something changed in you, and they begin to treat you differently, as well.

But let's be frank: this takes hard work. You're working on yourself, you're working on your attitudes, you're working on your personal relationships, and you're working on your professional goals, all at the same time. This isn't usually work that you'll get paid for, at least not directly; but if this work improves the value of your life experiences, then it is priceless. That's not to say that it's easy. It's not easy. Sometimes it's a pain in the ass. Sometimes you have to go outside your comfort zone; sometimes you have to put yourself out there in ways that leave you vulnerable to rejection and even mockery from others; sometimes you must endure the discomfort of dieting and even the physical pain of hard exercise; sometimes you have to cut ties with harmful people or habits, despite longstanding attachments and even a cherished part of your identity. Changing your life is not easy.

Many people who start on this journey eventually face setbacks they're unable to overcome; and then they bitterly describe the goals as unrealistic. But the greatest rewards are the outcome of a process. So pick your process, stick with it, and enjoy it.

The ultimate deciding factor in your quest for success is not your economic status, or your gender, or your race, or your personality, or your location. The ultimate factor is all in your mind. Have faith in yourself, and pursue work that is meaningful. Remember that your mistakes do not define you: they are learning opportunities, so learn what you can from them, and keep going.

If you wish to pursue success, then decide that you're the sort of person who's willing to keep trying after it gets difficult. You're willing to keep working towards your self-improvement goals despite setbacks and obstacles, not enough money, and people who try to discourage you, telling you that your dream is an unattainable delusion based on inspirational snake oil. Because chances are, someone you know will say something like that to you soon, if they haven't already: and perhaps, sometimes, that person may even be you. Ignore the naysayers. You achieve excellence by sticking with it over the long term.

As humans, we have trouble picturing the long term. Popular stories and movies show us the myth of "Ah ha!" moments, when a character's sudden realization results in a complete and instantaneous change. Here in reality, life doesn't work like that. In our quest for personal change, "Ah ha!" moments are necessary; but in and of themselves, they are not sufficient. **After a realization comes the hard work.** There will be inevitable backtracking and setbacks and frustration. We have to expect setbacks: otherwise the setbacks may begin to seem insurmountable when we encounter them. We have to keep working towards our goals, even if it takes the rest of our lives.

Hitting rock bottom, whatever that means in your life; or receiving a visitation from the Three Ghosts of Christmas, as Dickens imagined: can produce an "Ah ha!" moment which inspires you to want to change your life. But when you wake up the next morning after your revelation, the real work begins.

The truth is, it takes time.

Change doesn't happen all at once.

After you have decided to make a change in your life, you will almost inevitably become frustrated with the slow pace of change. Things won't go the way you want. There will be discomfort, possibly including physical pain, as you get your body back into optimum health. You might find yourself backsliding; I believe most of us do, at some point along our journey. You *will* feel like you've been working and working but you're yet to see results. It's inevitable. You've spent your whole life getting to this point; so changing direction can rarely be completely accomplished in a few short weeks. Make a commitment to treat this as a priority project for the long term. Don't beat yourself up if you can't change everything immediately.

Existing relationships with other people (including financial obligations, as well as social and familial ties); as well as our own ingrained habits and patterns of behavior: tend to pull us back into our unhealthy past, even if we don't want to go back. Changing in the face of these forces is like swimming against the current of a mighty river in flood. It's easier to get swept along, back into those same old unhealthy or unsatisfying roles that the other people in your life want you to have, regardless of what you want for yourself. Keep on swimming. Fight that current long enough, and eventually you'll get to a place where you can float along with less effort.

Make some choices a daily habit, and over time, the difference will be apparent to others, even if you're uncertain that you're seeing any results yourself. When you feel like you've been working forever without seeing any results, that is often the time *just before* other people start randomly complimenting you that you look good, or contacting you to make conversation for business or friendship. You are making progress. It just takes a long time. Give yourself time to make the change. Keep working on you, and you'll achieve the greatest work of your life.

And the good news is, sometimes getting started is the hardest part. (That's why starting today is so important!) Sometimes once you overcome a psychological barrier, you're able to move on to a point where doing difficult things no longer seems so insurmountable. Then you get to a point where doing difficult things is something you do all the time. It's still difficult! But you have conquered your own mind and transformed the way you look at things, and thus the greatest barrier was removed.

Sometimes all you have to do is ask. We worry and worry about rejection and hostility; but it turns out, other people are often willing to work with you and agree to your ideas if you just put yourself out there. Finding the courage to speak up is the hard part. That's the hurdle we must overcome. Sometimes we have to speak up repeatedly, or find a more effective way of communicating our concerns: but you are worth it! So speak up. Ask for what you want. You might be surprised at how well that works out.

As Jesus said:

"Ask, and it shall be given you; seek, and ye shall find; knock, and it shall be opened unto you." (Luke 11:9, also Matthew 7:7)

Sometimes, all you gotta do is ask; but first you have to work up the courage to say what you want. State it concisely. Say it repeatedly. Put yourself out there and ask for what you want out of life.

Sometimes the process of "seeking" involves a lot of hard work, perhaps even drudgery, before you "find" the goal of your quest, whatever it might be. And yet, even when we're washing dishes and plunging toilets, we can learn to be present in the moment and appreciate some aspect of this life, even now. And then you can get back on the path of living within your values, of living towards your purpose, of living your best life and being your best self.

5.2 Read more Self-Help Books

When you are done with this book, read another self-help book. When you are done with that one, pick up another. Become a self-help guru. (If you're the writing type, like me, then write your own self-help book!) The objective here is to change your thought patterns. A self-help book can show you a new direction, it can inspire you with a new light, it can reveal to you your own inner beauty and the grand potential of life. But after a few weeks, the world reasserts itself, and you begin to think all that self-help stuff was a load of crap after all.

Self-help is not a "one and done" activity. Yes, you might read a book that will change your life... for a little while; but if you're like most people, chances are that after some time has passed, old habits will creep back in. Some triggering event will occur, and you'll find yourself back in the downward spiral. I know that happened to me, more than once. That's because the act of reading a single book one time is insufficient, in and of itself, to cause a permanent change in your brain. If you're reading this book, then you probably have years, perhaps decades, of negative self-talk to overcome. I've said it before: Life is not a Hollywood movie. This is reality; and in reality, years-long ingrained habits of thought do not suddenly make a permanent snap into a completely different pattern after a single "ah ha!" moment. You need to keep having those moments of revelation, over and over, to really make a lasting change in your thought patterns.

If you really want to change your thought patterns, you have to immerse yourself in a new way of thinking over the long term. By feeding your mind a steady, ongoing stream of gratitude and self-help positivity over the course of several years, you can finally begin to reprogram your automatic responses, and begin to recognize the emergence of negative patterns earlier, so you can head them off, change your responses to stressful situations, and lead a happier, more relaxed, more joyful life.

5.3 Pursue Your Purpose

Your purpose is larger than any specific goal. Although we work towards different goals at different times, we may see, when we step back, that we've been working towards a larger purpose from various different directions for an entire lifetime.

Your sense of purpose may be difficult to put into words, but you can feel it in your gut when you are living in alignment with it.

Do more of what you love. Identify what you want in life, and state it clearly. Figure out the next steps that will be required in order for you to live the life you want to create for yourself; and then take those steps.

And once you've been trying it for a while, review your progress, and identify what is working well, and do more of that.

Follow your purpose, live your values, embody the best version of yourself, and enjoy a more fulfilling life.

Start today!

People Who Helped Make This Book Possible

I would like to express special thanks to Diana Usher, Vicki J. O'Grady-Longo, Dominick Domasky, Harry Spaight, Curtis Webster, Jr., Scott McCarthy, Chris Lalchan, Jason Robinson, Matt Hulbert, Rian Hansen, Mark Cumicek, and Joon Chang; to David, Cedar, and my amazing wife, Jessica Lehrfeld; and of course to my inspiring sister Lindsey LaRock and our mother, Jan Soloy, who modeled self-improvement and taught us how to love life. To all of you, and to so many more, thank you for your help and feedback and encouragement and patience while I was in the process of writing, editing, and living this book.

Recommended Reading

Among many other excellent resources, you may find the following titles fruitful in your own further pursuit of self-help subjects.[24]

Before Happiness by Shawn Achor

Change Your Brain, Change Your Life by Daniel Amen [I preferred the first edition]

The *Meditations* of Marcus Aurelius

Happier by Tal Ben-Shahar

Rising Strong by Brené Brown

Atomic Habits by James Clear

----

24 It doesn't really matter if you read the paperback or the hardcover or the e-book or listen to the audiobook: what matters is if their message connects with you and helps you in your own life.

The 4-Hour Work Week by Tim Ferris

The End of Dieting by Joel Fuhrman

Personality Isn't Permanent by Benjamin Hardy

Meditation for Fidgety Skeptics by Dan Harris and Jeff Warren

Peace is Every Step: The Path of Mindfulness in Everyday Life by Thich Nhat Hanh

Any and all other books by Thich Nhat Hanh

Switch: How to Change Things When Change Is Hard by Chip Heath and Dan Heath

The Creative Act by Rick Rubin

The Four Agreements by Don Miguel Ruiz

You Are A Badass by Jen Sincero

Tao te Ching (The Way of Life) by Lao Tzu. [For best results, read several different translations because they all tend to have unique interpretations of this book of ancient wisdom.]